Authoritative and readable, this brief survey is the first comprehensive historical overview of U.S. federal tax systems published since 1967. Its coverage extends from the ratification of the Constitution to the present day. Brownlee describes the five principal stages of federal taxation in relation to the crises that led to their adoption—the formation of the republic, the Civil War, World War I, the Great Depression, and World War II—and discusses the significant modifications during the Reagan presidency of the last stage.

Brownlee also addresses the proposals made since the fall 1994 congressional elections under the "Contract with America" and competing schemes, and he assesses today's conditions for a tax revolution in the light of the national emergencies that have produced revolutions in the past. While focusing on federal policy, Brownlee also attends to the related history of state and local taxation.

This historical account recognizes the power of democratic forces outside the government, the influence of institutions and expertise inside the government, and the potency of ideas as an independent creative force that may lend intention to democratic forces, governmental deliberations, and resulting policies. This "democratic-institutionalist" interpretation is a novel and major contribution to the history of taxation and public finance.

WOODROW WILSON CENTER SERIES

Federal taxation in America

Other books in the series

Michael J. Lacey, editor, *Religion and Twentieth-Century American Intellectual Life*

Michael J. Lacey, editor, *The Truman Presidency*

Joseph Kruzel and Michael H. Haltzel, editors, *Between the Blocs: Problems and Prospects for Europe's Neutral and Nonaligned States*

William C. Brumfield, editor, *Reshaping Russian Architecture: Western Technology, Utopian Dreams*

Mark N. Katz, editor, *The USSR and Marxist Revolutions in the Third World*

Walter Reich, editor, *Origins of Terrorism: Psychologies, Ideologies, Theologies, States of Mind*

Mary O. Furner and Barry Supple, editors, *The State and Economic Knowledge: The American and British Experiences*

Michael J. Lacey and Knud Haakonssen, editors, *A Culture of Rights: The Bill of Rights in Philosophy, Politics, and Law—1791 and 1991*

Robert J. Donovan and Ray Scherer, *Unsilent Revolution: Television News and American Public Life, 1948–1991*

Nelson Lichtenstein and Howell John Harris, editors, *Industrial Democracy in America: The Ambiguous Promise*

William Craft Brumfield and Blair A. Ruble, editors, *Russian Housing in the Modern Age: Design and Social History*

Michael J. Lacey and Mary O. Furner, editors, *The State and Social Investigation in Britain and the United States*

Hugh Ragsdale, editor and translator, *Imperial Russian Foreign Policy*

Dermot Keogh and Michael H. Haltzel, editors, *Northern Ireland and the Politics of Reconciliation*

Joseph Klaits and Michael H. Haltzel, editors, *The Global Ramifications of the French Revolution*

Continued on page following index

Federal taxation in America

A short history

W. Elliot Brownlee

WOODROW WILSON CENTER PRESS

AND

CAMBRIDGE
UNIVERSITY PRESS

Published by the Press Syndicate of the University of Cambridge
The Pitt Building, Trumpington Street, Cambridge CB2 1RP
40 West 20th Street, New York, NY 10011-4211, USA
10 Stamford Road, Oakleigh, Melbourne 3166, Australia

© 1996 by the Woodrow Wilson International Center for Scholars

First published 1996

Printed in the United States of America

Library of Congress Cataloging-in-Publication Data applied for

A catalog record for this book is available from the British Library.

ISBN 0-521-56265-1 hardback
ISBN 0-521-56586-3 paperback

For Mary Margaret

WOODROW WILSON INTERNATIONAL CENTER FOR SCHOLARS

The Center is the living memorial of the United States of America to the nation's twenty-eighth president, Woodrow Wilson. Congress established the Woodrow Wilson Center in 1968 as an international institute for advanced study, "symbolizing and strengthening the fruitful relationship between the world of learning and the world of public affairs." The Center opened in 1970 under its own board of trustees, which includes citizens appointed by the president of the United States, federal government officials who serve ex officio, and an additional representative named by the president from within the federal government.

In all its activities the Woodrow Wilson Center is a nonprofit, nonpartisan organization, supported financially by annual appropriations from Congress and by the contributions of foundations, corporations, and individuals.

WOODROW WILSON CENTER PRESS

The Woodrow Wilson Center Press publishes books written in substantial part at the Center or otherwise prepared under its sponsorship by fellows, guest scholars, staff members, and other program participants. Conclusions or opinions expressed in Center publications and programs are those of the authors and speakers and do not necessarily reflect the views of the Center staff, fellows, trustees, advisory groups, or any individuals or organizations that provide financial support to the Center.

Woodrow Wilson Center Press
Editorial Offices
370 L'Enfant Promenade, S.W., Suite 704
Washington, D.C. 20024–2518
telephone: (202) 287–3000, ext. 218

Contents

Acknowledgments

This book developed from a project of the Woodrow Wilson International Center for Scholars that studied the financing of the federal government since World War II. I am especially grateful to Michael J. Lacey, director of the Division of United States Studies at the Woodrow Wilson Center, for conceiving and organizing the project, and for pressing me to set the history of taxation and public finance in the broader history of American government and society. Edward Berkowitz, Hugh Heclo, Carolyn Jones, Cathie Martin, Stanford Ross, Herbert Stein, Eugene Steuerle, and Julian Zelizer were the other participants in the Woodrow Wilson Center project. They brought a wealth of experience and scholarly insight to bear on the history of taxation and public finance, and I found their advice invaluable.

Frank Smith, executive editor of Social Sciences at Cambridge University Press, and Joseph Brinley, director of the Woodrow Wilson Center Press, proposed that I write this book, and I am grateful for their encouragement. Their suggestions, as well as those of reviewers W. Andrew Achenbaum, Brian Balogh, and William J. Barber, greatly improved the final manuscript. Carolee

Belkin Walker, senior editor at the Woodrow Wilson Center Press, provided excellent editorial guidance and support.

The University of California remains superbly encouraging of scholarship. I am grateful to the Santa Barbara campus for sabbatical and various other important forms of support. Colleagues in the Department of History—Randolph Bergstrom, Mary Furner, Otis Graham, Carl Harris, Laura Kalman, Kenneth Mouré, and the late Robert Kelley—generously provided intellectual stimulation. I appreciated as well the comments of Michael Bernstein, Robert M. Collins, Peter Lindert, Richard Musgrave, Ed Perkins, Richard Sylla, and John Wallis on an overview of this book I presented at a conference on "Fiscal Crises in Historical Perspective" sponsored by the All-UC (University of California) Group in Economic History.

My largest debt of gratitude is to Mary Margaret Brownlee, who read virtually every draft of the manuscript. Her sharp critical eye saved me from numerous errors, and her historical insight suggested many fruitful lines of inquiry.

Santa Barbara
November 1995

Introduction

Taxation and national emergencies

The last fifteen years have witnessed the most profound changes in federal tax policy in peacetime since the New Deal of President Franklin Roosevelt. In 1981, the Economic Recovery Tax Act (ERTA), the first of the tax measures of the Reagan "revolution," helped finish what had been an "era of easy finance" under the tax system adopted during World War II. Also, ERTA propelled the federal government toward deficit finance—a move with greater impact than the one during the New Deal. The second of the Reagan measures—the Tax Reform Act of 1986—broadened the base of the income tax significantly but dramatically reduced the progressivity of its rate structure. The Reagan "revolution" did not abolish the income tax that had been crafted during World War II. Indeed, the tax remained the core of federal finance. But the revolution diminished the capacity of the income tax for raising revenue and shifted the criteria of fairness that guided the tax.

As the 1996 elections near, some of the architects of the "Contract with America" propose even more radical reforms, including eradicating the income tax as Americans have known it since 1913 and replacing it with either a national sales tax or the "flat tax." The flat tax would apply to the gross rather than the net incomes

1

of individuals, exempt interest and dividends from individual income taxation, exempt investments from corporate taxation, and eliminate a progressive rate structure.

Adoption of either the national sales tax or the flat tax would be a greater break with the past than was the 1913 ratification of the Sixteenth Amendment, which provided a constitutional basis for income taxation, and the adoption of income tax legislation in that same year. The income tax was a highly tentative experiment until World War I. Even the World War I tax system, which was based on income taxation, kept the central elements of the prewar system of tariffs and excises. In contrast, national sales tax and flat tax advocates would scrap virtually all of the central elements of the existing system of federal taxation. They would create a new tax regime—a new system of taxation with its own characteristic tax bases, rate structures, administrative apparatus, and social intentions.

In one sense, the history of tax regimes in America is not encouraging for radical reform in the 1990s. Thus far in American history, the federal government has infrequently adopted new tax regimes. The moments of sweeping change have come during the nation's great emergencies—the constitutional crisis of the 1780s, the three major wars, and the Great Depression. On the other hand, this same history suggests that Americans are capable of embracing drastic changes in their federal tax systems if the right political and economic circumstances converge. Characterizing Americans as relentlessly "antitax" in their political culture does not go very far toward explaining the complicated history of federal taxation, or providing an understanding of the capacity of the American political system to adopt new tax regimes—particularly during times of national crisis, as an essential part of the larger institutional pattern of crisis resolution. The architects of the flat tax and a national sales tax certainly claim that the nation is in the midst of a crisis of confidence in government that is forcing comprehensive reform of public institutions, including instruments of taxation.

This book emphasizes and examines the historic flexibility of the federal government in adapting its fiscal systems to social needs. The book delineates that flexibility in the context of explaining how and why the federal government crafted a distinct, new tax regime in each of the nation's great emergencies, and explaining how these regimes were linked to one another. A historical understanding of the political, economic, and intellectual underpinnings of American tax regimes may help evaluate the nation's current fiscal condition and the prospects for a shift to a new tax regime during the 1990s, whether under a flat tax or under some other reform measure. More importantly, this understanding of the history of taxation is intended to aid in explaining the enormous growth of the federal government, which, like the development of taxation, has hinged on the nation's great crises.

A summary of the history of federal tax regimes should begin with the great wars and their aftermaths. These wars—the Civil War, World War I, and World War II—were three of the five national emergencies, and the growth of the federal government was particularly dramatic during the wartime mobilizations. The tax regimes that helped finance these mobilizations proved to be crucial not only to the war efforts, which were unprecedented in scale, but also to the subsequent peacetime expansions of the federal government.

The federal government's need for vast new revenues to mobilize for great wars and, more generally, to meet national emergencies invariably forced its leadership to reexamine thoroughly the nation's financial options. In so doing, leaders faced issues that went far beyond the financial problem of meeting demands to increase government spending. The great crises—each of which involved the meaning or survival of the nation—stimulated debate over national values. At the same time, each of the great crises intensified ideological and distributional divisions within American society. Because wars required the sacrifice of lives as well as treasure, they were especially powerful stimulants of social division. The resulting political conflicts often centered on issues of taxation; tax politics was always an important vehicle for the expression of both national values and the underlying social and ideological conflicts that national emergencies intensified.

Within the economic and social turbulence of each crisis, the political leaders in the executive and legislative branches of government struggled to establish coherent tax policies. On the whole, crisis conditions strengthened the power of these leaders, and the tax systems they implemented further enhanced their influence. They mobilized party government and administrative techniques, including professional expertise, to expand the capacity and productivity of the federal tax system. To be sure, there was always tension between executive and legislative leaders over tax policy, and both the president and the Congress had to address the demands of local interests.

But during the Civil War and World War I, the common partisan loyalties and shared social values of the nation's political leaders largely overcame the pressures that tended to fragment American government. Consequently, during those two emergencies, the nation's political leadership created tax regimes with a high degree of coherence and intention.

Tension between the executive and the legislative branches, and the pressure of local interests, intensified during the 1920s and again during the late 1930s. Consequently, the administration of Franklin D. Roosevelt found it more difficult to influence the new tax regimes demanded by national emergencies than had the administrations of Abraham Lincoln and Woodrow Wilson. But appeals to party loyalty worked to Roosevelt's advantage, and he proved resilient in forging coalitions both inside and outside the federal government. As a result, the two tax regimes produced by the New Deal and World War II bore the imprint of his administration more than that of Congress, and the imprint of a national interest more than that of local interests.

Within the conflicted politics of each of the emergencies, the leaders of the federal government worked to persuade Americans to accept new taxes. During wartime, the architects of national mobilization made taxation part of larger strategies of persuading Americans to accept sacrifice. In the Civil War and each of the two world wars, they crafted new tax programs designed both to implement sacrifice and to convince the mass of taxpayers that their sacrifices were fair. In the process, the new tax systems acquired the symbolic function of expressing the goals of the federal government. The high-tariff system of the Civil War, for example, came to represent the commitment of the federal government to creating a powerful national market and to protecting capitalists and workers within that market.

To help make the case for fairness, the nation's political leaders experimented with progressive income taxes in the Civil War and then introduced them on a grand scale during the two world wars. The adoption of progressive taxes during those two wars took into account and exploited powerful impulses, stimulated by the forces of democracy and industrialization, for a restructuring of American society. As a consequence, both wars produced major advances in the cause of progressive taxation at the same time that they broadened the social and financial base for funding warfare and other purposes of the federal government.

During World War I, progressive impulses were so strong that the framers of tax policy launched major initiatives—especially the rigorous taxation of corporate excess profits—that were designed to democratize production and finance. The most radical initiatives did not survive the postwar reaction of the 1920s, but they continued to influence tax policy until World War II, when the requirements of unprecedented mobilization and the fear of post-war depression led the framers of progressive tax measures to focus on the taxation of the much larger base of salaries and wages, rather than that of rents, interest, and profits.

The tax regimes of the two world wars did not produce a social revolution. But they did establish tax policy that was far more progressively redistributional than it had been before World War I, establish a responsibility for the federal government to redistribute income according to ideals of social justice, and become a powerful expression of the democratic ideals of the nation.

The social tensions—tensions of class and section—created by industrialization might have led the nation eventually to adopt progressive income taxation even in the absence of war. But historical contingency played a powerful role. The wartime mobilizations and the fact that both mobilizations were managed by the leadership of the Democratic Party, which was more strongly committed to progressive income taxes and more opposed to regressive general sales taxes than the Republican Party, accelerated the process. In addition, by contributing to the resolution of wartime social crises, the emergency-driven tax policies acquired a legitimacy and cultural force that helped keep them in place well after the emergencies were over.

The opportunity to establish new taxes provided policy architects with openings to modernize the tax system, in the sense of adapting it to new economic and organizational conditions and thereby making it a more efficient producer of revenue. No process of "modernization" closely dictated the selection of options. But, in each crisis, policymakers discovered that the organizational maturing of industrial society had created a new menu of feasible options. Exploiting the new tax options during each emergency provided a structure and an administrative apparatus that allowed the federal government to capitalize effectively on postcrisis economic expansion.

By creating instruments of taxation that had acquired an independent legitimacy and were administratively more robust, each crisis opened up new opportunities for proponents of expanded government programs to advance their interests after the emergency was over. Postwar leaders were able to forge new expenditure programs—both direct and indirect—without incurring the political costs associated with raising taxes or introducing new ones. The popularity of the expenditure programs, in turn, reinforced the popularity of the tax system behind the programs. Thus, the crisis-born enhancement of tax capability contributed to the much discussed "upward ratchet" effect that emergencies had on government spending.

Each new tax regime drew political strength from the fact that it not only increased the size of the federal government but also increased the centralization of government. The relative growth of federal taxing was most rapid during the five national emergencies. To some extent, the expansion of federal taxing undercut the tax base of state government. But the federal government offset this and won state and local support for its tax regimes by assuming part of the burden of financing public services from states and localities after the crisis, and by finding ways to expedite the levying and collecting of state and local taxes.

The indirect expenditure programs were particularly important to the political survival of new tax regimes after national emergencies. The indirect programs, which are now known as "tax expenditures," were networks of privileges—deductions, exemptions, and credits—within the tax code. They resulted from the resurgence of local interests after the emergencies. These programs reduced tax bases and often made rate structures less progressive. But they left intact the fundamental intent of the emergency tax regimes. In fact, they provided significant political protection to the new regimes.

The survival of each emergency-born tax system in the postcrisis era lent the nation's tax system an increasingly layered, or diversified, quality. Each new regime preserved important elements of its predecessor—elements that had survived earlier postcrisis political tests. Thus, the World War II system contained not only the features that lent it distinction but also features that it inherited from the Civil War, World War I, and Great Depression regimes.

In the absence of a new national emergency, the systems of the early republic, the Civil War, World War I, and the New Deal might have survived much longer. Each of them produced revenues adequate for funding expansive postcrisis programs. Each of the systems faced substantial criticism, but in each instance political leaders developed successful strategies, including compromises in tax policy, for preserving the regime. Nonetheless, each tax system proved inadequate—both politically and economically—to meet the fiscal demands of a subsequent national emergency, and each gave way to a new system.

In the absence of a new national emergency, the World War II tax regime remains in place today, although its fiscal force and political legitimacy have become badly eroded. During the 1980s, the federal government, for the first time, embarked on comprehensive tax reform without facing a national emergency. It remains to be seen whether the reformed tax system will be adequate to meet the economic and political challenges facing the nation during the 1990s, and beyond. If it is not, the history of American tax regimes, including the conditions under which tax regimes formed and decayed, may suggest the contours of future—and possibly even more dramatic—reforms.

1

The formative tax regimes, 1789–1916

Modern American tax regimes began with the ratification of the U.S. Constitution in 1788. The new Constitution established powers and requirements that have had an enduring influence on future tax regimes. The Constitution gave the new federal government clear and broad powers to impose "indirect" taxes—taxes on commerce that consumers would pay only indirectly, through middlemen—as well as the power to borrow and the exclusive power to create money. But the Constitution restricted the ability to levy "direct" taxes—taxes levied directly on individuals. This restriction had a major impact on the form of future federal tax regimes and on the division of tax effort between the federal government and the governments of states and localities.

The framers of the Constitution provided only the skeleton of a state. It was up to the leaders of the new republic to develop the central instruments of government, including government finance. Those leaders experimented with many of the specific taxing instruments allowed by the Constitution, but they made extensive use only of the taxation of imports. They discovered that import taxes met most of their needs for tax revenues while minimizing political discord. Based on customs duties, the tax regime that followed the creation of the new constitutional order lasted until the Civil War, making that regime the longest in American history.

Only during the Civil War did politicians begin to exercise in earnest the wide range of tax instruments possible under the Constitution. As republican leaders forged the modern American nation-state, they greatly enhanced the scale and scope of modern public finance. The core of their wartime system of finance became an expression of national strength in the postwar era. Taken together, the framing of the Constitution and the fighting of the Civil War set the foundations for the tax systems that financed American nationhood during the twentieth century.

THE REGIME OF THE EARLY REPUBLIC

The fundamental structure of the federal tax system, as well as that of modern tax regimes, emerged from the formative emergency for the American state—the social crisis that extended from 1763 down to the formation of the U.S. Constitution. At its heart, the crisis was a constitutional struggle to define the basic ideas underlying the federal government: ideas of representation and consent, constitutionality and rights, and sovereignty.

At the same time Americans forged their ideas of government, they struggled with an array of practical problems. Among the most pressing were how to finance the Revolutionary War debts, and how to establish the credit of the nation in a way that would win respect in international financial markets. In the process of resolving problems that were both profound and mundane, the framers of the Constitution gave shape to the fiscal institutions they believed the new federal government—and a new nation— would need to survive and prosper.[1]

---

[1] For a survey of taxation during these formative years, one that "places taxation at the center of the movement that produced the Constitution" (p. 8), see Roger H. Brown, *Redeeming the Republic: Federalists, Taxation,*

The Constitution reflected the desire of James Madison, Alexander Hamilton, and its other leading supporters to provide the new central government with far greater capacity to tax than the Articles of Confederation government had enjoyed. The protracted fiscal crisis of the 1780s convinced Madison and Hamilton that the new representative government must have the fiscal power required to create a strong and meaningful nation. A central goal was to fund the debts that the Confederation and the states had inherited from the Revolutionary War, and to do so in a way that would win the confidence of those who were, or might become, creditors of the new government. In the process of funding the debts, the new government would both nurture and demonstrate the fiscal virtue of republican citizens. Consequently, while the Confederation could only exhort the states to contribute voluntarily to the federal treasury, the Constitution gave the new government the fiscal authority that would reflect its sovereignty. Congress had the general power, in the words of Article I, Section 8, "to lay and collect taxes, duties, imposts, and excises." In addition, Section 8 established the power "to borrow money on the credit of the United States" and "to coin money, regulate the value thereof, and of foreign coin."

The new fiscal powers, and especially the powers to tax and coin money, illustrated the trust in the new government held by the founders and the ratifiers of the Constitution. But another provision of the Constitution seemed to express worry about the taxing power. This was Article I, Section 9, which severely limited federal taxation of property. The clause specified: "No capitation, or other direct tax shall be laid, unless in proportion to the census."

and the Origins of the Constitution (Baltimore: Johns Hopkins University Press, 1993). The best survey of the concrete fiscal problems that were associated with financing the American Revolution, and that subsequently influenced the framers of the Constitution, is E. James Ferguson, *The Power of the Purse: A History of American Public Finance, 1776–1790* (Chapel Hill: University of North Carolina Press, 1961).

Identifying the basis for this limitation lies at the heart of interpreting the fiscal intentions of the framers of the Constitution. On
its surface, Article I, Section 9, might seem to express a Lockean
liberalism—a line of thinking that emphasized individualism, cele-
brated the pursuit of private self-interest and financial gain, and
regarded with suspicion any governmental initiatives that might
impede the search for individual gain. Much evidence with regard
to the general political culture of eighteenth-century America reinforces the interpretation that America was a society of profit-
maximizing tax resisters. Then, as now, numerous Americans of
all classes cheated, evaded taxes, exploited loopholes in the tax
code, migrated to low-tax havens, sought political groups and
representatives committed to reducing taxes, and welcomed constitutional restrictions on taxation. They became especially recalci-
trant during periods of economic adversity, such as the deflationary 1780s.

The major obstacle to this interpretation of Article I, Section 9,
is the fact that eighteenth-century Americans generally preferred
direct taxation—especially the taxation of property—to any other
form of taxation. Property taxation was almost everywhere the
instrument of choice for local governments. The limitation on the
federal government's use of property taxation had far more to do
with attitudes regarding the proper sphere of the federal government than it did with the scope of government in general or the
proper forms of taxation.

Understanding both the enthusiasm for property taxation at the
state and local levels and the worries about federal use of the
property tax requires recognition that the central language of the
Revolution contained much more than a Lockean liberalism, with
its emphasis on private rights. That language embraced as well
a classical republicanism, or a civic humanism, which stressed
communal responsibilities. These ideas focused on the threat of
corruption to public order, the dangers of commercialism, and the

need to foster public virtue. The founders, and even Adam Smith, held these ideas of classical republicanism in tension with those of liberalism.[2]

Commitments to civic humanism could create pressure for higher taxes, rather than lower. For example, the ideal of a harmonious republic of citizens equal before the law created demands for taxes to destroy islands of privilege by taxing the privileged more heavily. That ideal also embraced the notion that taxpaying was one of the normal obligations of a citizenry bound together in a republic by ties of affection and respect. This communal thinking went further, emphasizing the direct relationship between wealth and the responsibility to support government and public order. It embraced enlightened self-interest and included "ability to pay" as a criterion in determining patterns of taxation. In the first canon of taxation Adam Smith proposed in *The Wealth of Nations,* he declared that "the subjects of every state ought to contribute towards the support of the government, as nearly as possible, in proportion to their respective abilities." In an era when most wealth was in the form of real estate, the property tax—in particular, the taxation of property according to its value—became popular because it seemed to offer the greatest potential for taxing according to "ability to pay."

Property taxation was the mainstay of local government even in

---

[2] A useful introduction to the modern intellectual history of the Revolutionary era is found in the essays in Jack P. Greene, ed., *The American Revolution: Its Character and Limits* (New York: New York University Press, 1987). For important suggestions as to the long-run influence of civic humanism, see Dorothy Ross, "The Liberal Tradition Revisited and the Republican Tradition Addressed," in John Higham and Paul K. Conkin, eds., *New Directions in American Intellectual History* (Baltimore: Johns Hopkins University Press, 1979), 116–31. On Adam Smith as a civic humanist, see Donald Winch, *Adam Smith's Politics: An Essay in Historiographic Revision* (Cambridge: Cambridge University Press, 1978).

the colonial period, but after 1775 states began to employ it extensively. The democratic forces unleashed by the American Revolution fueled movements throughout America to reform state taxation. Often these movements focused on abandoning deeply unpopular poll taxes and shifting taxes to wealth as measured by the value of property holdings. The accomplishments of these reform movements varied widely across the new states, and the development of new property taxes stalled during the hard deflation of the 1780s. But even conservative elites began to understand the potential of property taxation to raise revenue and quell social discord. Proponents of tax reform worried that the new national government might preempt the use of property taxation by state and local governments. Thus, restricting the national government's ability to levy property taxes represented an expression of civic humanism.[3]

The limitation on the federal use of direct taxation also reflected the fact that the framers of the Constitution thought about taxation in the context of the corruption of the British Parliament and the monarchy and sought to prevent similar abuse by the new federal government. They believed that local control was necessary for the equitable operation of the property tax. The federal government, they feared, might become too far removed from the people or captured by a powerful faction. The consequence might be abuse of the property tax. The framers who were associated with a particular industry or section of the country often worried that the federal government might single out their industry or section for discriminatory property taxation. Slaveowners, for example, worried about federal property taxation that would single out slave property. Representatives of rural districts worried about

[3] The complicated story of tax reform during the American Revolution is ably told by Robert A. Becker, *Revolution, Reform, and the Politics of American Taxation, 1763–1783* (Baton Rouge: Louisiana State University Press, 1980).

taxation that might favor town dwellers over farmers. An example of such taxation was the taxation of property holdings on the basis of their acreage rather than their value. Urban commercial interests worried about the reverse—federal taxation of property holdings on the basis of their value.

Such fears, in turn, fueled the fear of factionalism that James Madison, a civic humanist, expressed in *Federalist* No. 10. He predicted that "the most common and durable source of factions" would be "the various and unequal distribution of property." He concluded that the issue of taxation, more than any other, created an opportunity and temptation for "a predominant party to trample on the rules of justice." Madison regarded the large scale of the republic as the fundamental protection against factionalism, but in his mind Article I, Section 9, provided additional security. Lending even further protection was the requirement of Article I, Section 8, that "all duties, imposts, and excises shall be uniform throughout the United States." This clause prevented Congress from singling out a particular state or group of states for higher rates of taxation on trade, and reflected the hope of Madison and his *Federalist* coauthor Hamilton that the new Constitution would foster the development of a national marketplace.

Madison and the other framers of the Constitution did not regard Article I, Section 9, as crippling the new federal government. Indeed, they were confident that Article I, Section 8, established the means for the new government to acquire the economic resources it needed to fulfill its promise. They believed that the Constitution, even with the limitation, left the way open for the new federal government to raise the tax revenues it needed through indirect taxes—taxes such as tariffs and excises, which the federal government collected indirectly, by intermediaries such as merchants.

Tariffs, in fact, turned out to provide the core of federal finance, beginning with legislation enacted in 1789 and expanded under the financial program of the first secretary of the treasury, Alexander Hamilton. During the 1790s, these taxes applied relatively low rates to a great range of imports. The consequent revenues accounted for about 90 percent of total federal tax revenues between 1789 and 1815.[4]

The revenues from tariffs enabled the federal government to assume the state debts, consolidate existing federal debt, and thereby establish the public credit of the new federal government. In particular, the new tax revenues demonstrated that the federal government could service its debt from current revenues. In the critical 1790s, tax revenues more than covered the federal government's interest payments on the national debt, despite the fact that they accounted for more than half of federal expenditures—a larger share than at any time since, including the most dramatic national emergencies.

The revenue system proved adequate for almost all the other needs of the new federal government. It needed virtually no tax revenues to carry out two of its most important economic functions—maintaining a customs union and distributing the public lands. (Public-land sales roughly covered the costs of administering the land system.) But for other important activities, the new government did require tax revenues. It used indirect taxes to finance the undeclared naval war with France in the late 1790s and Jefferson's war against the Barbary pirates. Tariff revenues, in combination with the debt finance that the general taxing power made possible, funded the Louisiana Purchase. Tariff revenues, along with land subsidies, allowed presidents from Thomas Jefferson through John Quincy Adams to implement the ambitious program

---

[4] Bureau of the Census, *Historical Statistics of the United States: Colonial Times to 1970,* Part 2 (Washington, D.C.: U.S. Government Printing Office, 1975), 1106.

of internal improvements designed by Albert Gallatin, Jefferson's secretary of the treasury. The federal government had paid off all its debt by 1836, and in 1837 customs duties also enabled President Martin Van Buren's treasury to undertake a major distribution of surplus revenues to the states for internal improvements.[5]

From 1789 through the War of 1812, the most heated controversies regarding taxation concerned excise taxes, rather than tariffs. Excises turned out to arouse the very factionalism that Madison had feared because they seemed to single out unfairly particular classes of producers. President Washington and Secretary Hamilton discovered this after Congress, in 1791 and 1792, followed their recommendation and enacted the nation's first excise taxes—ones that applied to distilled spirits. Despite the fact that Congress structured the tax to favor whiskey production at the expense of rum production, the tax touched off the Whiskey Rebellion of 1794. President Washington had to raise 15,000 troops to discourage the Pennsylvania farmers who had protested, waving banners denouncing tyranny and proclaiming "Liberty, Equality, and Fraternity."[6]

The protest ended any substantial Federalist interest in excise taxation. But Hamilton and other leading Federalists wanted to wield all the taxing powers provided by the Constitution. In 1792, Hamilton explained to Washington that enactment of the whiskey

---

[5] For a survey of federal taxation in the early national period, see Henry Carter Adams, *Taxation in the United States, 1789–1816* (Baltimore: Johns Hopkins University Press, 1884). No twentieth-century historian has written a survey of taxation, let alone public finance, in the early national period, but a political scientist has made a useful effort for the federal government. See Dall W. Forsythe, *Taxation and Political Change in the Young Nation, 1781–1833* (New York: Columbia University Press, 1977).

[6] See Thomas P. Slaughter, *The Whiskey Rebellion: Frontier Epilogue to the American Revolution* (New York: Oxford University Press, 1986).

excise was desirable so that "the authority of the National Government should be visible in some branch of internal Revenue; lest a total non-exercise of it should beget an impression that it was never to be exercised & next that it ought not to be exercised."[7]

Hamilton and Washington had a dual purpose. For one thing, they were preparing, in particular, for wartime and international crises during which trade might be inadequate for the revenue needs of the federal government. For another, they were promoting taxpaying as an expression of republican citizenship, and even of loyalty to a new nation. But, in the wake of the Whiskey Rebellion, Hamilton understood the popular hostility to excises. The Federalists experimented further with excises, but limited them almost exclusively to goods and services consumed by the affluent. These taxes included a kind of luxury tax on carriages, a stamp tax on legal transactions, and a tax on snuff.

The Federalists also wanted to exercise the power to levy direct taxes. In 1798, to help finance the naval buildup against France, the Federalists enacted a direct tax on property and assigned revenue goals to the states on the basis of population. Once again, to blunt the reaction to the distributional effects of the tax, the Federalists gave it a progressive twist. They required each state, in raising its share of revenue, to tax houses at rates that increased as the value of the houses increased.

None of the Federalist experiments with more progressive forms of excise or direct taxes worked well, except to establish precedents for future tax initiatives. The measures raised little revenue and, even in their progressive form, contributed to Federalist political defeats in 1798 and 1800. Subsequently, in 1802, the Jefferson administration led in the abolition of all excise and direct taxation.

---

[7] Hamilton to Washington, August 18, 1792, *The Papers of Alexander Hamilton,* Harold C. Syrett, ed. (New York: Columbia University Press, 1967), Volume 12, 236–7.

Prospects were dismal for using internal taxes to demonstrate republican commitment to the new federal government.

As the federal government removed itself from the realm of direct taxation, state and local governments forged ahead with the development of revenue systems that relied heavily on property taxes. Most dramatic was the use of property taxation by state governments. Two fundamental forces—the democratization of politics and the industrialization of the economy—accelerated the property-tax movement. As the Industrial Revolution gathered force during the 1820s and 1830s, Jacksonian reformers extended the scope of property taxation, trying to tax all forms of wealth. By the Civil War, they had created in most states the elements of a general property tax designed to reach not only real estate, tools, equipment, and furnishings, but also intangible personal property such as cash, credits, notes, stocks, bonds, and mortgages. Some states simply expanded the statutory definitions of what constituted property for tax purposes. Other states added to their constitutions provisions for uniformity (requiring that properties of equal value be taxed at the same rate) and for universality (requiring that all property be taxed). For example, Ohio's 1851 constitution provided that "Laws shall be passed taxing by a uniform rule all moneys, credits, investments in bonds, stocks, joint-stock companies or otherwise; and also all real and personal property, according to its true value in money" (Article 12, Section 2). Ohio had launched general property-tax reform as early as 1825 and had garnered sustained increases in taxes on personal property. But, empowered by its 1851 constitution, in only two years the state doubled its assessment of personal property—to about two-thirds the value of real property. In the same two-year period, both state and local tax collections nearly doubled.

By the 1860s, in much of the nation, property taxation was the dominant source of state and local revenues. As a consequence of the apparent success of property taxation for state and local purposes, state and local political leaders became increasingly vigilant in watching for possible federal incursions into their property-tax base.[8]

After the federal government withdrew from direct and excise taxation, it relied primarily on tariffs for its revenue needs. Low tariffs proved to be a great financial success. Low tariffs produced revenue in periods of expanding foreign trade, which began as early as the 1790s, when American merchants profited handsomely from the Napoleonic Wars. Economic growth, which began to increase in a significant and sustained way during the 1820s, meant continuing increases in the per capita demand for imported goods and, in turn, increases in tariff revenues per capita. The flow of most ocean commerce through a few major ports provided the setting for well-administered tariffs. Low tariffs proved inexpensive to collect, and their collection did not require force.

Low tariffs were also a political success. When tariff rates were low, they won popularity. Other advantages proved important as well. Low tariffs were widely diffused or more general in their

---

[8] For overviews of the antebellum reform movement for general property taxation, see Sumner Benson, "A History of the General Property Tax," in George C. S. Benson, et al., *The American Property Tax: Its History, Administration, and Economic Impact* (Claremont, Calif.: Claremont Men's College, 1965), 31–52, and Richard T. Ely, *Taxation in American States and Cities* (New York: Thomas Y. Crowell, 1888), 131–45. On Ohio's property-tax experience, see Ely, 146–59 and 456. The major exceptions in the increasing reliance by state governments on property taxation were in the South, where the waxing movement to protect slavery increasingly shielded slaves from state taxation. In North Carolina, for example, during the 1840s and 1850s the state government relied on investment income from banks and railroads and on borrowing to reduce its reliance on property taxes. See Richard Sylla, "Long-Term Trends in State and Local Finance: Sources and Uses of Funds in North Carolina, 1800–1977," in Stanley L. Engerman and Robert E. Gallman, eds., *Long-Term Factors in American Economic Growth*, National Bureau of Eco-

scope; they did not seem to penalize particular groups the way excises did. Taxes on imported luxury goods seemed to tax extravagant living, and tariffs were useful in economic diplomacy. To almost all Americans, the tariffs seemed a legitimate and reasonable exercise of power by the new government. In short, low and moderate tariffs allowed the leaders of the early republic to limit the political divisiveness of taxation. In their effort to create a republic that was both strong and just, the early American leaders relied on relatively low tariffs to raise substantial revenues yet prevent tax issues from arousing disruptive forces of factionalism.

The nation's leaders broke from the reliance on low tariffs on only two occasions. One was the War of 1812, when a sharp decline in foreign trade ruined customs revenues. Congress responded by reviving excise taxation and, in 1813, by imposing a direct tax assessment on the states. The federal government, following Article I, Section 9, assigned it to the states according to population; each of the states, in turn, generally met its revenue assessment by a state property tax allocated to counties according to the distribution of taxable property. In all, taxation financed more than 40 percent of wartime expenditures, and the war was so popular that there was no significant political backlash to the temporarily high levels of taxation. No permanent changes in either the level or the kind of federal taxation emerged from the war.

The other break with low tariffs came during a period of experimentation with protectionism that began in the 1820s and lasted until the early 1830s. Industrialization promoted the goal: protecting America's high-wage workers and high-cost industries as

nomic Research, *Studies in Income and Wealth,* Volume 51 (Chicago: University of Chicago Press, 1986), 832–5. Another valuable state-level study is Peter Wallenstein, *From Slave South to New South: Public Policy in Nineteenth-Century Georgia* (Chapel Hill: University of North Carolina Press, 1987).

they learned how to meet their British competition. The major departure in this direction came in 1824, when Congress levied a 35 percent tax on imported iron, woolen, and cotton goods. The act also increased tariffs on imported raw materials, including flax, hemp, iron, lead, molasses, and raw wool.

But protection had little beneficial effect on American industries, most of which had developed on their own the ability to compete with their British counterparts. Moreover, Southern planters and Western farmers generally resisted measures that seemed to increase the price of manufactured goods. Southern politicians, especially in South Carolina, denounced the 1828 tariff legislation as the "Tariff of Abominations" and vowed to overturn it in the future, one way or another. In addition, during the Nullification Crisis of 1832–33, high tariffs came to symbolize federal power for South Carolinians worried about the future of slavery.

Consequently, in 1833 Congress began to reduce tariffs, enacting a measure that provided for a gradual, biennial reduction of the tariff so that by 1842 rates would return to the modest levels set in 1816. In 1846, Congress passed the Walker Tariff, which reduced tariffs even further; only lip service to the principle of protection remained. The Walker Tariff paralleled Britain's repeal of the Corn Laws in the same year, and it seemed to herald the adoption of free trade throughout the Anglo-American world.

The Mexican War began in the same year that Congress adopted the Walker Tariff. Financing the war demonstrated once again the enormous revenue potential of low customs duties in a period of economic expansion. The economic recovery that had begun in the early 1840s, coupled with the lower import duties, produced an upsurge in federal revenues that enabled the federal government to pay for the war without any increase in tax rates or any introduction of new taxes. Tax revenues covered more than 60 percent of wartime expenditures, and the continued buoyancy of customs duties enabled the federal government to have nearly paid off its Mexican War debts by the time of the Civil War. The nation could look forward to funding future wars of territorial or imperial expansion in a similar fashion—so long as those wars were not substantially larger in scope and did not disrupt the federal government's ability to raise revenue through international trade.

Had it not been for the Civil War, changes in the tax policies of the federal government might well have been minimal during the rest of the nineteenth century. Low tariffs for revenue, the borrowing power that Secretary Hamilton's financial program had helped establish, and the enormous landed resources of the federal government would probably have been adequate to meet the needs of the federal government if a great national emergency had not intervened.

THE CIVIL WAR REGIME

The Civil War was the first great national emergency. In fact, it may well have been the crucible for modern American nationhood. It certainly transformed government and its revenue systems. It was the nation's first modern war in the sense of creating enormous requirements for capital. Union war costs drove up government spending from less than 2 percent of the gross national product to an average of 15 percent, close to the 20 percent level reached in the early 1990s. The capital requirements evoked a program of emergency taxation that was unprecedented in scale and scope. That emergency program extensively employed all the taxes provided for by the framers of the Constitution.[9]

---

[9] For suggestions of the significance of the Civil War to the meaning of the American nation, see Carl Degler, "One among Many: The United States and National Unification," in Gabor S. Boritt, ed., *Lincoln, the War President: The Gettysburg Lectures* (New York: Oxford University Press, 1992), 91–119.

Broad electoral support within the North enabled the newly dominant Republican Party to meld its interests with those of the federal government and achieve a great deal of latitude in setting national tax policy. Despite the dramatic break with the modest liberal state of the past, Republican leaders did not face significant resistance to the huge new taxes or need to rely on coercion for their collection. The Republicans were able to persuade the American public to accept the massive broadening of the fiscal foundation of the federal government. Taxpaying became a way for Americans to demonstrate their loyalty to the Union government and to the American nation.

The Republicans introduced a tax system composed primarily of high tariffs and excise taxes, which had been so unpopular during the early republic. These new taxes funded about 20 percent of wartime expenditures. Republican Congresses increased tariffs every year during the war, and the Tariff Act of 1864 imposed duties that were almost half the total value of all dutiable imports.[10] They also imposed excise taxes on virtually all consumer goods. To administer these taxes, in 1862 Republicans created the office of the commissioner of internal revenue. The first commissioner, George S. Boutwell, described the office as "the largest Government department ever organized."[11] During and after the war this system of consumption taxation became the centerpiece, in turn, for the Republicans' ambitious new program of nation-building and national economic policy.[12]

---

[10] The standard history of tariff legislation remains Frank W. Taussig, *The Tariff History of the United States* (New York: G. P. Putnam's Sons, 1931).

[11] George S. Boutwell, *Reminiscences of Sixty Years in Public Affairs,* Volume I (New York: Greenwood Press, 1968 reprint), 313.

[12] On the ways in which the Republicans powerfully fused the interests of party, the state, and the nation during the Civil War, see Richard F. Bensel, *Yankee Leviathan: The Origins of Central State Authority in*

The Republican consumption taxes were regressive, taxing people with lower incomes at higher rates than those with higher incomes. Republican leaders generally preferred such taxes, but they also recognized that regressive taxes might undermine confidence in the Republican Party and the war effort, particularly in western and border states. Consequently, they looked for a supplementary tax that bore a closer relationship to "ability to pay" than did the tariffs and excises. The twin goals would be to raise additional tax revenue, thus easing inflationary pressures, and to convince taxpayers that the wartime fiscal system was fair.

The leadership had few options. The rudimentary accounting methods followed by homes, farms, and businesses meant that the most practical method to raise huge amounts of revenue quickly was the one they had already chosen: taxing goods at the point of importation or sale. Even this approach required the swift development of a large administrative apparatus for the collection of excises.

Less practical, but perhaps feasible, was adapting the administrative systems that state and local governments had developed for property taxation. Secretary of the Treasury Salmon P. Chase and Thaddeus Stevens, chair of the House Ways and Means Committee, favored this approach at first, and they proposed an emergency property tax modeled after one adopted during the War of 1812. But virtually everyone regarded a property tax as a "direct" tax, and Article I, Section 8, of the Constitution required the federal government to allocate a direct tax among the states on the basis of population rather than property values. Members of Congress from western states (including the Great Lakes states), border states, and poorer northeastern states protested that this would mean a higher rate of taxation on property in their states.

America, 1859–1877 (Cambridge: Cambridge University Press, 1990), 1–237.

They also complained that the tax as written would not reach the personal property held as real estate improvements and as "intangibles" such as stocks, bonds, mortgages, and cash. Congressman Schuyler Colfax of Indiana declared, "I cannot go home and tell my constituents that I voted for a bill that would allow a man, a millionaire, who has put his entire property into stock, to be exempt from taxation, while a farmer who lives by his side must pay a tax."

In response to the complaints, the leadership took note of how the British Liberals had used income taxation in financing the Crimean War as a substitute for heavier taxation of property. Justin S. Morrill of Vermont, who chaired the Ways and Means Subcommittee on Taxation and was a staunch proponent of high tariffs, introduced a proposal for a new and very different tax—the first federal income tax. Congressional leaders viewed the tax as an indirect tax because it did not directly tax property values.[13]

The first income tax was ungraduated, imposing a basic rate of 3 percent on incomes above a personal exemption of $800. Amendments in subsequent war years reduced the exemption and introduced mild graduation. In 1865, the tax imposed a 5 percent

---

[13] The most informative scholarship detailing the development of income-tax legislation between the Civil War and World War I remains Roy G. Blakey and Gladys C. Blakey, *The Federal Income Tax* (London: Longmans, Green, 1940), 1–103; Sidney Ratner, *American Taxation: Its History as a Social Force in Democracy* (New York: Norton, 1942), 13–340; and Edwin R. A. Seligman, *The Income Tax: A Study of the History, Theory, and Practice of Income Taxation at Home and Abroad* (New York: Macmillan, 1914). Robert Stanley has revised this scholarship, emphasizing the conservative forces behind the development of the federal income tax through 1913. In explaining the adoption of the first federal income tax, he emphasizes the Republican desire to provide political protection for the consumption-based tax regime. See Robert Stanley, *Dimensions of Law in the Service of Order: Origins of the Federal Income Tax, 1861–1913* (New York: Oxford University Press, 1993).

rate on incomes between $600 and $5,000 and 10 percent on incomes over $5,000. The rates seem low by twentieth-century standards, but they imposed higher taxes than the wealthy of the mid-nineteenth century were used to paying under the general property tax.[14] The tax reached well into the affluent upper-middle classes of the nation's commercial and industrial centers. The administrative machinery created by the commissioner of internal revenue relied heavily on the cooperation of taxpayers, but compliance was high, prompted by patriotic support for the war effort and by the partial enactment of British "stoppage at the source" (meaning collection at the source or the withholding of taxes by corporations and others who make payments of income). The commissioner of internal revenue lacked the administrative capacity to obtain earnings reports or collect taxes from farms and small businesses, where most Americans earned their income. But the law did require corporations—railroads, banks, and insurance companies, primarily—to collect taxes on dividends and interest, which constituted a large share of the income of the affluent citizens the law was designed to tax. Also, the law required agencies of the federal government to collect taxes on salaries, which grew substantially during the wartime mobilization.

By the end of the war, more than 10 percent of all Union households were paying an income tax, and the rate of taxpaying probably reached 15 percent in the northeastern states, where the federal government collected three-fourths of its income-tax revenues. These households probably constituted roughly the slice of society that economic historians have estimated as owning 70 percent or more of the nation's wealth in 1860. The income base for taxation was so substantial that in 1865 the tax, even with its low rate, produced nearly $61 million—21 percent of the federal

---

[14] For evidence that propertied New Yorkers paid substantially higher income taxes than property taxes, see Seligman, *The Income Tax,* 473–5.

tax revenues for that year. (The various excises accounted for 50 percent and the tariffs the remaining 29 percent.) With the end of hostilities and the resumption of full-scale foreign trade, customs revenues more than doubled in 1866, but income-tax revenues still accounted for 15 percent of all tax revenues. (The share of customs duties rose to 37 percent while the share of excises fell slightly, to 48 percent.)[15]

The Republican wartime government built the kind of revenue system necessary to establish a powerful modern state. But the rudimentary administrative apparatus available for direct taxation essentially prevented the Lincoln administration from financing a much larger share of the war through tax revenues. Even so, taxes, almost all of them new, financed about one-fifth of Union war costs.[16]

During the late 1860s and early 1870s, Republican Congresses

[15] These estimates are based on the well-known data on taxpayers developed by the commissioner of internal revenue for 1866. By contrast with my emphasis, Robert Stanley, citing a figure of only 1.3 percent of the American people paying income taxes, claims that the tax did not reach the middle class. Stanley arrives at a lower number, and a serious underestimate of the social reach of the income tax, by including the Confederate population and by not estimating taxpaying households. See Stanley, *Dimensions of Law in the Service of Order*, 39–40 and 263–4. On estimates regarding the distribution of income and wealth, 1790–1860, see W. Elliot Brownlee, *Dynamics of Ascent: A History of the American Economy* (New York: Alfred A. Knopf, 1979), 134–6.

[16] In addition to imposing broad-based taxes, the Union government borrowed from the middle class as well as from the wealthy and created a functional money supply. Critiques of the borrowing and monetary policies of Secretary of the Treasury Chase abound. See, for example, Robert A. Love, *Federal Financing: A Study of the Methods Employed by the Treasury in Its Borrowing Operations* (New York: Columbia University Press, 1931), 74–117. For a more positive view of Chase, see John Niven, *Salmon P. Chase: A Biography* (New York: Oxford University Press, 1995).

phased out most of the excise taxes, which the general public resented in peacetime and blamed for postwar increases in the cost of living. Abolishing the excise taxes made it easier for the Republican leadership to phase out the income tax as well. Congressional Republicans generally wanted to respond to the demands of the extremely affluent citizens, who had accepted the income tax only as an emergency measure and now lobbied vigorously to ensure first the reduction of the tax and then its discontinuance at its sunset date of 1870. Little organized support emerged for permanent income taxation, and only a minority of the party's congressional leadership thought about the tax as a valuable rhetorical shield to protect regressive tariffs. Fewer still actually liked the distributional effects of the tax. Consequently, beginning in 1867, the Republican leadership increased the exemptions and lowered the rates. In 1870, Congress—mistakenly fearing a deficit—extended the tax, but then allowed it to expire in 1872.

Republicans, however, maintained the consumption basis of the federal tax system by keeping two elements of the Civil War tax system. First, they retained the high tariffs. Frequent revisions of the tariff schedules left intact the fundamental structure of the tariff system. Until the Underwood-Simmons Tariff Act of 1913 significantly reduced the Civil War rates, the ratio between duties and the value of dutiable goods rarely dropped below 40 percent and was frequently close to 50 percent. The highest rates were imposed on manufactured goods—particularly metals and metal products, including iron and steel, cotton textiles, and certain woolen goods. On many manufactured items the rate of taxation reached 100 percent. By 1872, tariff duties dominated federal revenues; except in a few years of severe depression and during the financing of the Spanish-American War, they would do so until 1911.

Second, Republicans left in place the taxes on alcohol and

tobacco products and a few taxes on luxury items such as perfumes and cosmetics. Buoyant, price-inelastic demand for alcohol and tobacco products meant that taxes on them yielded substantial revenues, even after the federal government reduced the tax rates. In the years before World War I, revenues from levies on alcohol and tobacco always produced at least one-third of all federal tax revenues, and by the mid-1890s they averaged close to one-half. During 1911–13, alcohol and tobacco taxes produced even more revenue than did the tariffs.

The Republican taxes worked politically and survived into the postwar period, despite their regressiveness, partly because, like consumption taxes in general, they escaped the notice of many taxpayers. But at least as important was the fact that the taxes won public acceptance, for a variety of reasons. Most critically, the new tax regime had acquired political momentum by helping to finance a war that defined the meaning of the American nation. For most of northern society, the Union victory had enhanced the legitimacy of Republican tax measures and, more generally, its program of nationalist state-building and economic development.

Important as well to the acceptance of the taxes was the popularity of the programs they funded. After the Civil War the consumption-tax regime financed popular military operations, including the early phases of Reconstruction in the South, the continuing warfare with Native American tribes, and the initiation of a modern navy. Most of the tax revenues that financed the Spanish-American War came from a doubling of the taxes on tobacco and alcohol products.

Broadly popular new programs of public works and transfer payments were also all visibly financed by consumption taxes. These federal programs rewarded loyalty to the Union cause and to the Republican Party. Community leaders throughout the North became accustomed to feeding from what became known as the "pork barrel"—the annual Rivers and Harbors Bill that the consumption-tax revenues funded. Republican governments also used consumption taxes to fund the nation's first major system of social insurance: an ambitious program of pensions and disability benefits for Union veterans and their dependents.

As the pensions grew decidedly generous during the 1880s and 1890s, they became a central element in the strength of the Republican Party and continued to be important politically and economically into the twentieth century. Disbursements for disability and old-age benefits, all funded from consumption taxes, soared after the 1879 Arrears Act and the 1890 Dependent Pension Act liberalized benefits. The benefit spending remained at a high level until World War I, and during the late 1890s the pensions required about 45 percent of all federal receipts. The taxes that funded the transfer payments were regressive, but the distribution of benefits was progressive—at least within the states of the victorious Union. The portion of the American population who received Civil War pensions, especially in northern states, compared well with the levels provided by the German and Danish old-age systems, although it fell short of the level provided by British old-age pensions before World War I. In addition, the Americans who were in the Civil War benefit system enjoyed terms of coverage, such as eligibility for benefits, that were reasonably generous when compared with those offered by European social programs.[17]

State and local governments, particularly when under the control of Republicans, welcomed the government centralization that the new social programs created. State and local leaders appreciated the way in which the programs satisfied demands for public

---

[17] See William H. Glasson, *Federal Military Pensions in the United States* (New York: Oxford University Press, 1918), and Theda Skocpol, *Protecting Soldiers and Mothers: The Political Origins of Social Policy in the United States* (Cambridge, Mass.: Harvard University Press, 1992), 102–51. See 130–5 for the international comparisons.

works and welfare that they would otherwise have had to meet. During the 1880s and the first decade of the twentieth century, urbanization accelerated significantly, requiring cities to invest more in parks, schools, hospitals, transit systems, waterworks, and sewers. State governments increased their investments in higher education and began to aid localities in financing schools and roads.

The federal programs were especially welcome because they indirectly relieved the beleaguered system of property taxation that state and local governments employed. Industrialization and economic instability after the Civil War undermined the egalitarian promise of the general property tax to tax all wealth at the same rate. The self-assessment procedures commonly used were inadequate to expose and determine the value of cash, credits, notes, stocks, bonds, and mortgages, especially in the nation's largest cities. The insensitivity of assessment procedures to changes in price level increased the inequities during the economic crises of the late nineteenth century. State and local governments began to develop the modern property tax, with its standardized assessment practices and its focus on real estate.[18]

The consumption-tax system remained popular also because of its regulatory dimensions. The enactment of the system represented a stunning victory for economic protectionism and, more generally, for government regulation through taxation. The Republican consumption-tax system made tax incentives (and disincentives) and tax subsidies important, popular, and permanent elements in the federal revenue structure.

---

[18] On the complex difficulties with the general property tax, see Clifton K. Yearley, *The Money Machines: The Breakdown and Reform of Governmental and Party Finance in the North, 1860–1920* (Albany: State University of New York Press, 1970), 3–95 and 137–65.

The high excise taxes on alcohol and tobacco appealed to much of the middle-class population as discouragements to, and punishments for, the consumption of commodities thought to be sinful and threatening to a virtuous republican social order. At the same time, the distilling and brewing industries valued the taxes because they provided legitimacy and meant tacit support from the federal government in the struggle against prohibitionist forces.

American business leaders lauded the regulatory effects of the tariff system. Manufacturers welcomed the protection they believed the tariffs afforded them against foreign competitors, and they praised the tendency of a favorable trade balance with Europe to encourage capital formation in America. During the 1870s and 1880s, manufacturers became especially enthusiastic about the high-tariff system because it allowed them to build national marketing organizations, free of worries about disruptions caused by European competitors. The high tariffs provided benefits not so much to the infant industries favored by Adam Smith as to the giant American corporations that were integrating vertically and gaining a long-term advantage over their European competitors, who were restricted to smaller markets.

Bankers and members of the financial community generally favored less emphasis on protection, more attention to the stimulation of international trade, and reductions in spending on lighthouses and pensions, coupled with further tax reductions. Nonetheless, they liked the way in which substantial taxes on consumption forced increases in the nation's rate of saving and facilitated the repayment of the wartime debt. By using consumption taxes to finance the war debt and interest payments (the latter rendered in the gold collected by customs duties), the Republican leadership transferred significant amounts of capital from consumers to holders of federal debt (Europeans as well as Americans), who tended to be wealthier than the average consumer and more likely to invest. And creditors, especially the holders of the federal debt, appreciated the way in which the Republican taxes tended to produce budget surpluses in the 1870s, reduced the debt, helped to contract the money supply, and eased the return to the domestic gold standard in 1879.[19]

High tariffs also seemed to benefit workers, who commonly feared competition from lower-wage labor in Europe, Latin America, and Asia and favored tax policies that advanced the prosperity of their industries. Labor support for the high-tariff position of the Republican Party had much to do with its smashing victory in the "critical election" of 1896 and its strong electoral displays, which continued until the Great Depression.

Finally, the high-tariff system received vigorous support from congressional leaders for purely political reasons. They discovered that the tariff system created significant opportunities for them to reinforce or enhance their power. By making adjustments within the complex and poorly understood web of tax subsidies, congressional politicians could offer benefits to narrowly defined groups or threaten these groups with penalties, without fear of fatal reprisal from larger publics.

The Republican architects of the tax regime, however, had to face significant partisan resistance to their tax policy, especially after the resumption of serious two-party competition. During the 1870s and 1880s, the Democratic Party challenged Republican power with a biting critique of a central element of the consumption-tax system—the tariff. To some extent, sectional interests drove the Democratic challenge. It was an appeal to the

---

[19] One estimate is that debt retirement and interest payments accounted for as much as half of the rise of the share of national economic product devoted to capital formation between the 1850s and the 1870s. See Jeffrey G. Williamson, "Watersheds and Turning Points: Conjectures on the Long-Term Impact of Civil War Financing," *Journal of Economic History*, 34 (September 1974): 636–61.

southerners who received neither the regulatory nor the programmatic benefits—Civil War pensions, for example—of the tariffs and excises they paid. But the critique was a more general attack on special privilege, monopoly power, and public corruption—one that harked back to the ideals of the American Revolution and the early republic. The Democrats described the tariff as the "mother of trusts" and, more generally, as the primary engine of a Republican program of subsidizing giant corporations. The Democrats framed their message to appeal to southerners, to be sure, but also to farmers, middle-class consumers, and owners of small businesses throughout the nation.

In fact, during the 1880s and 1890s, the two competing political parties came to base their economic appeals on sharply conflicting ideological views of the tariff and of taxation in general. In a kind of path-dependent politics initiated by the Civil War crisis, those party identities would have a major influence on revenue policy until World War II. The Republicans' invocation of high tariffs and the Democrats' response had sharply polarized the parties on issues of taxation. These tax issues would exacerbate class conflict for nearly a century.[20]

Criticism of the tariff intensified during the depression of the mid-1890s. Economic distress stimulated Populists in the West and the South, and champions of Henry George's "single tax," who were scattered throughout urban America, to promote social justice through tax reform. These two movements converged in their efforts to find ways to use the tax system to punish and discourage monopoly power. The Populists championed a progressive tax on the profits of corporations and the incomes of the wealthy, and single taxers often supported it at the federal level

---

[20] On the partisan and ideological nature of the tariff debates, see Tom E. Terrill, *The Tariff, Politics, and American Foreign Policy, 1874–1901* (Westport, Conn.: Greenwood Press, 1973), especially 210–7.

while they sought radical reform of the property tax at the state and local levels.[21]

The new grassroots pressure began to change the politics of federal taxation. During the Civil War, the Republican leadership had exercised a great deal of discretion in crafting the income tax. To be sure, they had developed the tax in anticipation of sectional and class resistance to a federal property tax. But they had designed the tax without any group's insistence that they do so. And, after the war, they set their own timetable for its demise. In contrast, when Congress began to seriously reconsider income taxation during the early 1890s, it did so primarily in response to popular pressure. Moreover, Congress then faced numerous proposals for a high degree of progression, and the proposers' arguments had a sharp, radical edge.

Central to the appeal of a highly progressive income tax during the 1890s was the claim that the tax would both reallocate fiscal burdens according to "ability to pay" and help restore a virtuous republic free of concentrations of economic power. The rhetoric was, in a sense, conservative; it directed attention to the values of the early republic. What was potentially radical about the movement for progressive income taxation was its content: the goal of raising the government's revenues primarily or even entirely from the largest incomes and corporate profits. The radical advocates for income taxation argued that their tax would not touch the wages and salaries of ordinary people but would, instead, attack unearned profits and monopoly power. The tax would, its proponents claimed, redress the wealth and power maldistribution that was responsible for the evils of industrialization. Those who be-

---

[21] The traditional "progressive" scholarship placed a great deal of emphasis on the importance of such grassroots pressure by farmers in shaping the inception of the federal income tax. See, for example, Elmer Ellis, "Public Opinion and the Income Tax, 1860–1900," *Mississippi Valley Historical Review* 27 (September 1940): 225–42; and Ratner, *American Taxation*, passim.

lieved they had faced expropriation would now do the expropriating.

Thus, support for a radical progressive income tax had far more to do with the search for social justice in an industrializing nation than with the quest for an elastic source of revenue. The tax became an integral part of democratic statism—a radical program of invoking instruments of government power to create a more democratic social order. This redistributional aspect of democratic statism was a major theme uniting some of the important legislative initiatives undertaken by the federal government before World War II. It was, in part, a new kind of liberalism, a realignment of classic nineteenth-century liberalism and the commonwealth tradition of early republicanism, which included a distrust of commerce. Democratic statists like the Populists and the single taxers regarded themselves as applying the ideals of the American Revolution to the new conditions of industrial society. Although the strategy remained one of liberating individual energies by providing a social order of abundant opportunity, the tactics had changed. To these new liberals, the state had become a necessary instrument and ally, not an enemy. They designed their tax program to restructure the market-driven machinery for distributing income and wealth.[22]

[22] For a discussion of the meaning of democratic statism and its relationship to progressive income taxation, see W. Elliot Brownlee, "Economists and the Formation of the Modern Tax System in the United States: The World War I Crisis," in Mary O. Furner and Barry E. Supple, eds., *The State and Economic Knowledge: The American and British Experiences* (Washington, D.C.: Woodrow Wilson Center Press; Cambridge: Cambridge University Press, 1990), 401–35. Democratic statism also had an expression in the regulatory taxation of individual and corporate behavior. In this regard, after the turn of the century, reformers built on the precedents of alcohol and tobacco taxation and used the federal taxing power to regulate grain and cotton futures, the production of white phosphorous matches, the consumption of narcotics, and even the employment of child labor. See R. Alton Lee, *A History of Regulatory Taxation* (Lexington: University Press of Kentucky, 1973).

During the severe economic depression of the mid-1890s, the pressures for progressive tax reform from western and southern Populists became strong enough to begin a shift in the position of the leadership of the Democratic Party. A contributing factor was the decline of foreign trade and tariff revenues during the depression. This enabled the Democrats to embrace a proposal for a new tax while still calling for the shrinkage of swollen Republican programs. Democrats took control of both houses of Congress in 1893, and their leaders in the House from the South and the West, including Benton McMillin of Tennessee, who chaired the Ways and Means Subcommittee on Internal Revenue, enacted an income tax in 1894 as part of the Wilson-Gorman Tariff. They sensed an opportunity to use tax issues for a major realignment of the two political parties along sectional and class lines, and they debated the income tax with unprecedented agrarian ferocity.[23]

Hostility from northeastern Democrats, as well as the opposition of most Republicans (including leaders, like Senator John Sherman of Ohio and Senator Justin Morrill of Vermont, who had supported the Civil War income tax), limited the progressivity of the tax. Within both parties, leaders recalled how effective the Civil War income tax had been in reaching the incomes of the nation's wealthy families. Congress reproduced many of the technical features of the Civil War income tax but established a much higher personal exemption ($4,000) and a somewhat lower rate on incomes and profits (2 percent). In any event, the 1894 tax was

---

[23] For suggestions of this kind, see Charles V. Stewart, "The Federal Income Tax and the Realignment of the 1890s," in Bruce A. Campbell and Richard J. Trilling, eds., *Realignment in American Politics: Toward a Theory* (Austin: University of Texas Press, 1980), 263–87. Stewart also describes the way in which political parties, in building consensus, moderated the content and rhetorical tone of income-tax proposals after 1896. See Stewart, "The Formation of Tax Policy in America, 1893–1913" (Ph.D. dissertation, University of North Carolina at Chapel Hill, 1974).

short-lived. In 1895 the Supreme Court, in *Pollock v. Farmers'
Loan and Trust Co.*, declared that the income tax of the Wilson-
Gorman Tariff was unconstitutional.[24]

The *Pollock* decision raised a significant institutional barrier to
progressive taxation, but it also stimulated some support for income taxation. Populists and Democrats from the South and the
West now attacked the Court and found that their audiences
responded enthusiastically. Democrats began to introduce constitutional amendments that would permit income taxation, and in
1896 the Democratic Party formally endorsed income taxation.
This was the first time a major party had done so.

But the Democrats went down to a decisive defeat in 1896, and
the Republican Party's leaders believed the results proved that they
need not feel any urgency in confronting pressure for progressive
tax reform. When Republicans faced the problem of financing the
Spanish-American War in 1898, they had recovered the power to
neutralize the Democratic thrust for income taxation, and they did
so with confidence.[25]

---

[24] Modern scholarship has modified an older "progressive" interpretation of
the *Pollock* decision as a conspiratorial act of judicial fiat. For that view,
see Robert G. McCloskey, *The American Supreme Court* (Chicago: University of Chicago Press, 1960), 140–1, and Sidney Ratner, *Taxation and
Democracy in America* (New York: Wiley, 1967), 193–214, among others. The best current discussion of the role of the Court is Stanley, *Dimensions of Law in the Service of Order*, 136–75. Stanley argues that the
Court was engaged in a kind of Jacksonian attack on the dominant role of
Congress in "statist capitalism." Consistent with his interpretation is Morton Horwitz's argument that the *Pollock* decision was a logical culmina-
tion of a process that established an "anti-redistributive principle" as
"part of the very essence of the constitutional law of a neutral state." See
Morton J. Horwitz, *The Transformation of American Law, 1870–1960:
The Crisis of Legal Orthodoxy* (New York: Oxford University Press,
1992), 19–27.

[25] For suggestions of the influence on tax policy of what political scientists
call "critical elections" on tax policy, see Susan B. Hansen, *The Politics of*

During the next fifteen years, however, support for income taxation grew gradually. The gains were most marked across rural America but especially strong in the Midwest and the West. Republican leaders like Robert M. La Follette of Wisconsin discovered that income taxation was one of those reform issues that attracted and held voters to the alignment the party had crafted in 1896. Presidents Theodore Roosevelt and William Howard Taft both recognized this support and made vague gestures on behalf of a graduated income tax (in 1906 and 1908, respectively). But popular backing for income taxation grew too in the urban Northeast; both Republican and Democratic leaders found that the tax had begun to appeal to their constituents.

Important to the new support for federal income taxation was the formation of an urban-rural alignment of middle-class citizens who favored state and local tax reform. The economic depression of the 1890s, followed by accelerating demands for services from state and local governments, accentuated the flaws in general property taxation. Both farmers and middle-class property owners in towns and cities resented how their tax burdens grew as a consequence of the inability of local and state governments to use general property taxation to reach intangible personal property. And these groups became interested in the adoption of new taxes—such as income, inheritance, and corporate taxes—as replacements for state property taxes.[26] Small property owners, both

Taxation: Revenue without Representation (New York: Praeger, 1983). Hansen rests heavily on these elections, which produced long-term realignments of party loyalty, for explaining the timing of major shifts in tax policy, but the fit is very loose. Among the critical elections, only the 1860 (and possibly 1980) election was followed by an immediate shift in tax regimes; the 1896 election confirmed the existing regime rather than ushering in a new one; and the introduction of the World War I regime was not associated with a critical election.

26 For an example of early advocacy for replacing personal property taxation with state income taxation, see Ely, *Taxation in American States and Cities*, 287–311.

rural and urban, increasingly believed that income taxes would help restore the progressiveness lost in the administrative collapse of the Jacksonian general property tax under industrial conditions.[27]

But states were very slow to adopt the new, alternative taxes, and industrial states were especially slow in adopting income taxes. Administrative difficulties and fears of damaging industry and jobs discouraged them. Nonetheless, the debates promoted widespread interest in any approach, including adoption of income taxes, that might rebalance the equity of the tax system. In addition, the sluggish progress of income taxation at the state level increasingly convinced middle-class citizens that it would be desirable to enact the tax at the federal level.[28]

During the ferment over tax issues at the state and local levels, some defenders of the wealthiest property owners joined in support of federal income taxation. They concluded that the tax might

[27] See David P. Thelen, *The New Citizenship: Origins of Progressivism in Wisconsin, 1885–1900* (Columbia: University of Missouri Press, 1972), 202–22; Yearley, *The Money Machines*, 193–250; John D. Buenker, *Urban Liberalism and Progressive Reform* (New York: W. W. Norton, 1973), especially 103–17; and Morton Keller, *Regulating a New Economy: Public Policy and Economic Change in America, 1900–1933* (Cambridge, Mass.: Harvard University Press, 1990), 208–15.

[28] In 1911, Wisconsin adopted the first modern income tax. The state finessed the administrative problems by collecting most of the revenues from corporations, which faced a stringently administered 6 percent tax on their profits. Manufacturers accounted for about two-thirds of the corporate burden. Massachusetts and New York did not adopt income taxes until they faced the fiscal problems imposed by World War I, and until they were confident that they could build the administrative machinery required to assess and collect a tax based primarily on individual incomes rather than corporate profits. Most industrial states did not enact income taxes until the revenue crisis created by the Great Depression. For the history of the Wisconsin income tax, see W. Elliot Brownlee, *Progressivism and Economic Growth: The Wisconsin Income Tax, 1911–1929* (Port Washington, N.Y.: Kennikat Press, 1974).

help take the wind out of the sails of more radical tax measures at the state and local levels. The most influential among these conservatives was a group of urban economists and attorneys who were tax experts. Edwin R. A. Seligman of Columbia University and Charles J. Bullock of Harvard University led them in promoting income taxation, on the one hand, and in moderating the rhetoric used to justify the tax, on the other. As early as 1894 Seligman had argued that the point of the tax was to "round out the existing tax system in the direction of greater justice." Such language helped shift the discourse over taxation from a focus on the salvation of industrial America to an emphasis on a moderate redistribution of the tax burden.[29]

Conservative support for moderate income taxation might be described as expressing a kind of "corporate liberalism," or "progressive capitalism." More generally, this vision, developing in tension with democratic statism, influenced not only the development of income taxation but also the ideas of the so-called progressive movement. Reformers of this more conservative persuasion wanted to bring a greater degree of order to industrial society and to strengthen national institutions, just as did the democratic statists. But, in contrast with democratic statists, "progressive capitalists" or "corporate liberals" looked with admiration on the efficiency of the modern corporation. Government regulation, including taxation, was desirable only if it served to protect the investment system.[30]

By 1909, there were enough insurgent Republicans in Congress

[29] Edwin R. A. Seligman, "The Income Tax," *Political Science Quarterly* (1894): 610.

[30] Exemplary discussions of corporate liberalism are Mary Furner, "Knowing Capitalism: Public Investigation and the Labor Question in the Long Progressive Era," in Furner and Supple, eds., *The State and Economic Knowledge*, 241–86, and Martin J. Sklar, *The Corporate Reconstruction of American Capitalism, 1890–1916* (Cambridge: Cambridge University Press, 1988).

who supported a graduated income tax to force action. A diverse group of representatives and senators from both parties supported the immediate enactment of such a tax. Congressman Cordell Hull, a first-term Democrat who represented the same Tennessee district as had Benton McMillin, noted changes in the composition of the Supreme Court and found it "inconceivable" that the nation "had a Constitution that would shelter the chief portion of the wealth of the country from the only effective method of reaching it for its fair share of taxes."[31] A bipartisan group hammered out a proposal, but they had to limit the progressiveness of the tax in order to generate enough support. Senator Nelson Aldrich, the chair of the Senate Finance Committee, proved resourceful in both preserving Republican Party union and blunting the thrust toward income taxation. He worked closely with President Taft to persuade the insurgents to accept a modest corporate income tax, described as "a special excise tax." He also worked to submit the Sixteenth Amendment, legalizing a federal income tax, to the states for ratification. Aldrich and the northeastern Republicans recognized the growing popular support for income taxation but hoped that the measure would fail.

Ratification prevailed in 1913, much to the surprise and consternation of standpat conservatives.[32] The process of ratification succeeded in part because of two other campaigns. One was a revival of the single-tax movement. Beginning in 1909, soap magnate Joseph Fels, who had converted to Henry George's faith in the single tax, began to finance campaigns for constitutional reforms permitting classification of property for the purpose of taxation (and thus high rates of taxation on the "site value" of land)

---

[31] Cordell Hull, *The Memoirs of Cordell Hull*, Volume 1 (New York: Macmillan, 1948), 49.

[32] The standard source on the ratification movement is John D. Buenker, *The Income Tax and the Progressive Era* (New York: Garland, 1985).

and local option in taxation. Although the campaigns won no significant electoral victories except in Oregon in 1910, they awakened the interest of the urban middle class in using the income tax to redistribute wealth.[33] The campaigns also convinced more wealthy property owners that they needed moderate reform as a defensive measure, and their support was important to the crucial victory of ratification in New York in 1911. The other set of campaigns was the presidential election of 1912. As a consequence of the campaigns of Woodrow Wilson, Theodore Roosevelt, and Eugene Debs, popular enthusiasm for federal policies designed to attack monopoly power reached an all-time high.

In 1913, bipartisan support for income taxation was broad, and the Democrats controlled Congress. Nonetheless, the income tax measure they enacted was only modest. To some extent this was because the leaders of both parties were cautious and wanted to maximize support for income taxation within the Northeast, where they feared the tax would be unpopular, and thus maintain party unity. To a greater extent it was because the nation's political leaders, as well as the general public, were unsure of how much redistribution they wanted the new tax instrument to accomplish. Woodrow Wilson urged caution on Furnifold M. Simmons, chair of the Senate Finance Committee. "Individual judgments will naturally differ," Wilson wrote, "with regard to the burden it is fair to lay upon incomes which run above the usual levels."[34] Moreover, the supporters of income taxation were themselves uncertain how

---

[33] On Joseph Fels's campaigns see Arthur P. Dudden, *Joseph Fels and the Single-Tax Movement* (Philadelphia: Temple University Press, 1971), 199–245, and Arthur N. Young, *The Single Tax Movement in the United States* (Princeton: Princeton University Press, 1916), 163–83.

[34] Woodrow Wilson to Furnifold M. Simmons, September 4, 1913, in Arthur S. Link, ed., *The Papers of Woodrow Wilson,* Volume 28 (Princeton: Princeton University Press, 1978), 254.

income ought to be defined or how the income tax would work administratively.

Finally, virtually none of the income-tax proponents within the government believed that the income tax would become a major, let alone the dominant, permanent source of revenue within the consumption-based federal tax system. Certainly the advocates of income taxation who were hostile to the protective tariff hoped that the tax would succeed and expedite reduction of tariffs. But they doubted that the new revenues would be substantial. And the idea that the tax would enable the federal government to grow significantly was far from the minds of the drafters of the 1913 legislation.

To be sure, Congressman Hull, who was the primary drafter of the 1913 legislation, wanted to make certain that the federal government would have access to the income tax in wartime; he believed that the federal government could make the tax, as an emergency measure, even more productive than it had been during the Civil War. But for Hull, as well as for the other income-tax enthusiasts, the revenue goals of the tax were far less important than the desire to use the tax to advance economic justice.[35]

---

[35] Jordan A. Schwartz has cited Cordell Hull's emergency-revenue argument in claiming that "anticipation of war made the income tax a war tax." See Schwartz, *The New Dealers: Power Politics in the Age of Roosevelt* (New York: Alfred A. Knopf, 1993), 14. There is no evidence, however, that Hull expected war in 1910, when he made the cited comment, and there is much evidence that Hull was then primarily interested in a redistribution of tax burdens. For Hull's own description of his important role in federal tax reform before World War I, see Hull, *Memoirs of Cordell Hull*, 45–74. Between 1894 and 1913, when champions of income taxation referred to the possible need to levy it in wartime, they were usually buttressing their legal arguments for the constitutionality of the federal tax. See, for example, the dissenting opinion of Justice John Marshall Harlan in *Pollock v. Farmers' Loan and Trust Company*, 158 U.S. 601,

Consequently, the Underwood-Simmons Tariff Act of 1913, which reestablished the income tax, was less progressive and less ambitious in its revenue goals than the Civil War legislation or even the legislation of 1894. The new tax established the "normal" rate of 1 percent on both individual and corporate incomes, with a high exemption ($3,000 for single taxpayers) that excused virtually all middle-class Americans from the tax. The tax also established a graduated surtax up to 6 percent, but this did not come into play for incomes under $20,000. In the first several years of the income tax, only about 2 percent of American households paid taxes. Meanwhile, the tariff and the taxation of tobacco and alcohol remained the most productive sources of revenue. The tariff, in fact, became even more productive because the 1913 reduction of tariff rates by the Wilson administration stimulated trade and increased revenues. If it had not been for World War I mobilization, the major consequence of the passage of the income tax in 1913 might have been the protection of the regime of consumption taxation inherited from the Civil War.

15 S.Ct. 673, 39 L.Ed. 1108 (1895), and Edwin R. A. Seligman, "The Proposed Sixteenth Amendment to the Constitution," in Seligman, *The Income Tax,* 627–8. (Seligman first published this part of his essay in 1910.) Historians have only rarely claimed that the architects of the Sixteenth Amendment or the 1913 legislation expected the tax to produce major additions to federal revenue. The leading examples are Ben Baack and Edward J. Ray, who claim that the passage of the 1913 income tax "signaled voters that the federal government had the wherewithal to provide something for everybody." See Baack and Ray, "The Political Economy of the Origin and Development of the Federal Income Tax," in Robert Higgs, ed., *Emergence of the Modern Political Economy: Research in Economic History, Supplement 4* (Greenwich, Conn.: JAI Press, 1985), 121–38.

2

The democratic-statist tax regimes,
1916–1941

By the time of World War I, the forces of industrialization had abundantly fueled democratic pressures for the federal government to enter the arena of direct taxation and assume some of the responsibility that state and local governments had undertaken for ameliorating social tensions over the uneven distribution of wealth. At the same time, mature industrialization, which included the flowering of modern corporations and of sophisticated financial intermediaries, had created much of the organizational capability necessary for implementing a direct tax on the incomes of corporations and wealthy individuals. But even so, the federal government would have been slow to adopt income taxation without the play of historical contingency. Without the intervention of the United States in World War I and the management of that intervention by the leaders of the Democratic Party, the development of federal taxation would have proceeded far more incrementally. It almost certainly would have relied much more heavily on the taxation of consumption.

As it was, the highly contingent politics of mobilizing for World War I drove the creation of a democratic-statist tax regime. That regime, with its steeply progressive tax rates and its tax base consisting of the incomes of corporations and wealthy individuals, provided the core of wartime finance. The regime then endured and survived the return to "normalcy" after World War I. The democratic-statist thrust of federal taxation weakened under the economic and political pressures that the highly progressive rate structure created for carving out loopholes. But in a contingent fashion, another national emergency—this one economic, in the form of the Great Depression—intervened. Once again, the leadership of the Democratic Party was in a position to manage the crisis, and the administration of Franklin D. Roosevelt resumed the democratic-statist restructuring of the federal tax system that had begun during World War I. Following that approach, the New Deal launched a new tax regime.

THE WORLD WAR I SYSTEM

The financial demands of World War I, set in the context of redistributional politics, accelerated tax reform far beyond the leisurely pace that corporate liberals would have preferred. In fact, the wartime crisis produced a brand-new tax regime—one that was close to the ideals of democratic statists. This new tax system, the most significant domestic initiative to emerge from the war, probably would not have taken the form it did had the United States not entered the war.[1]

---

[1] On the financing of World War I, see W. Elliot Brownlee, "Wilson and Financing the Modern State: The Revenue Act of 1916," *Proceedings of the American Philosophical Society* 129 (1985): 173–210; Brownlee, "Economists and the Formation of the Modern Tax System in the United States: The World War I Crisis," in Furner and Supple, eds., *The State and Economic Knowledge;* and Brownlee, "Social Investigation and Political Learning in the Financing of World War I," in Michael J. Lacey and Mary O. Furner, eds., *The State and Social Investigation in Britain and the United States* (Washington, D.C.: Woodrow Wilson Center Press; Cambridge: Cambridge University Press, 1993), 323–64. See also Jerold L. Waltman, *Political Origins of the U.S. Income Tax* (Jackson: University

The tax-reform process began in 1916 when President Wilson and Secretary of the Treasury William G. McAdoo made the single most important financial decision of the war. They chose to cooperate with a group of insurgent Democrats in arranging wartime financing on the basis of highly progressive taxation. Led by Congressman Claude Kitchin of North Carolina, who chaired the House Ways and Means Committee, the insurgent Democrats attacked concentrations of wealth, special privilege, and public corruption. Kitchin exploited the influence of the Ways and Means Committee. The Democratic insurgents were able to insist that if preparedness, and later the war effort, were to move forward, they would do so only on the financial terms of the insurgents. They embraced taxation as an important means to achieve social justice according to the humanistic ideals of the early republic. Redistributional taxation then became a major element of the Wilson administration's program for steering between socialism and unmediated capitalism.[2]

Press of Mississippi, 1985). For a different interpretation of World War I finance, see economist Charles Gilbert, *American Financing of World War I* (Westport, Conn.: Greenwood Press, 1970). Gilbert was interested in World War I finance as an example of how democracies tend to abstain from the kind of taxation that would promote strategic mobilization with the least inflation and disruption of productive capacity: taxation transferring purchasing power from consumers to the government. "War finance," Gilbert wrote, "is and always has been a victory of expediency over economics" (236). Gilbert's characterizations of tax institutions are similar to those of the political scientists described as pluralists. Herbert Stein presented a more positive view of McAdoo's Treasury but offered one similar criticism of its approach to taxation. Stein suggested that the Treasury was unwilling to pay the political costs of devising a tax program focused on discouraging "nonessential production." See Herbert Stein, *Government Price Policy in the United States during the World War* (Williamstown, Mass.: Williams College, 1939), 78–84 and 124.

[2] Southern sectionalism reinforced the class-based populism of Claude Kitchin. Some political-science scholarship has stressed the crippling effect of post–Civil War Southern sectionalism, and the associated hostility toward the federal government, on the development of a modern state. But this

The war provided an opportunity for Democratic progressives to focus the debate over taxation on one of the most fundamental and sensitive economic issues in modern America: What stake does society have in corporate profits? More specifically, the question became one of whether the modern corporation was the central engine of productivity, which tax policy should reinforce, or whether it was an economic predator, which tax policy could and should tame. The outcome of the debate was that the nation embraced a new tax system: "soak-the-rich" income taxation.[3]

Thus, during the period of crisis, one in which the pressure of fighting a modern war coincided with powerful demands to break the hold of corporate privilege, Wilson and the Democratic Party turned Republican fiscal policy on its head. They embraced a tax policy that they claimed—just as the Republicans had for their tariff system—would sustain a powerful state and economic prosperity. But the new tax policy of the Democrats was one that

scholarship does not discuss progressive federal income taxation, which, if anything, this sectionalism (expressed in the careers of Claude Kitchin and Cordell Hull) promoted during World War I. See Richard Bensel, *Sectionalism and American Political Development, 1880–1980* (Madison: University of Wisconsin Press, 1984); Bensel, *Yankee Leviathan*; and Jill Quadrango, *The Transformation of Old Age Security: Class and Politics in the American Welfare State* (Chicago: University of Chicago Press, 1988). Historians are well aware of the general significance of the Southerners who were in the Wilson administration or among his supporters in Congress, but no one has systematically examined their ideas on government. The best analyses are Arthur S. Link, "The South and the 'New Freedom': An Interpretation," *The American Scholar* XX (1950–1): 314–24; and George B. Tindall, *The Emergence of the New South, 1913–1945* (Baton Rouge: Louisiana State University Press, 1967), 1–60.

[3] A contrasting view of the importance of redistributional impulses is John Witte's. In explaining the crucial Revenue Act of 1916, he stresses the "dictates of war" and asserts that "there is little evidence of an independent interest in redistributing income through the tax system." See John Witte, *The Politics and Development of the Federal Income Tax* (Madison: University of Wisconsin Press, 1985), 81–2.

assaulted, rather than protected, the privileges associated with corporate wealth.

The Democratic tax program, implemented in the wartime Revenue Acts, transformed the experimental, rather tentative income tax into the foremost instrument of federal taxation. The Democratic program introduced federal estate taxation. It imposed the first significant taxation of corporate profits and personal incomes but rejected moving toward a more broadly based income tax— one falling most heavily on wages and salaries. Last but far from least, it adopted the concept of taxing corporate "excess profits." Alone among all the World War I belligerents, the United States placed excess-profits taxation—a graduated tax on all business profits above a "normal" rate of return—at the center of wartime finance. Excess-profits taxation turned out to be responsible for most of the tax revenues raised by the federal government during the war. Taxes accounted for a larger share of total revenues in the United States than in any of the other belligerent nations, despite the fact that by the end of 1918 the daily average of war expenditures in the United States was almost double that in Great Britain and far greater than that in any other combatant nation.[4]

The income tax with excess-profits taxation at its core outraged

---

[4] A comprehensive explanation of differences among the belligerents in their reliance on taxation would have to incorporate economic constraints as well as political culture. The explanation would have to recognize, for example, that while Great Britain financed somewhat less of its war costs through taxation (roughly 29 percent as against 37 percent for the United States), Britain's war costs were about 21 percent larger than those of the United States. Gerd Hardach provides limited international comparisons regarding war finance. See Hardach, *The First World War, 1914–1918* (Berkeley: University of California Press, 1977), 150–5. The source behind most of Hardach's figures is Harvey E. Fisk, *The Inter-ally Debts: An Analysis of War and Post-war Public Finance, 1914–1923* (New York: Bankers Trust Company, 1924). The most careful accounting of American war costs remains Edwin R. A. Seligman, *Essays in Taxation* (New York: Macmillan, 1921), 748–82.

business leaders. Redistributional taxation, along with the war-time strengthening of the Treasury (including the Bureau of Internal Revenue, the forerunner to the Internal Revenue Service), posed a long-term strategic threat to the nation's corporations. Those most severely threatened were the largest corporations, which believed their financial autonomy to be in jeopardy. In addition, the new tax system empowered the federal government, as never before, to implement egalitarian ideals. No other single issue aroused as much corporate hostility to the Wilson administration as did the financing of the war. Wilson's long-time supporters within the business community, among them Bernard Baruch, Jacob Schiff, and Clarence Dodge, bitterly attacked his tax program within the administration and often quietly supported Republican critics. The conflict between advocates of democratic-statist, soak-the-rich taxation on the one hand and business leaders on the other hand would rage for more than two decades.

Despite the damage to business confidence, the Wilson administration and congressional Democratic leaders moved forward with excess-profits taxation with almost no attention to the complaints of Baruch and other business critics. The Democratic leaders did so in part because they shared Kitchin's ideal of using taxation to restructure the economy according to nineteenth-century liberal ideals. They presumed that the largest corporations exercised inordinate control over wealth and that a "money trust" dominated the allocation of capital. For Wilson and McAdoo, the tax program, with its promise to tax monopoly power and break monopoly's hold on America's entrepreneurial energy, seemed to constitute an attractive new dimension to Wilson's "New Freedom" approach to the "emancipation of business." Thus, wartime public finance was based on the taxation of assets that democratic statists regarded as ill-gotten and socially hurtful, comparable to the rents from land monopolies that Henry George and his followers had wanted to tax. In fact, both Wilson and McAdoo entertained explicit single-tax ideas as they developed their tax-reform program.[5]

Party government also played a crucial role in the decision of the Wilson administration. Wilson and McAdoo knew they could have easily engineered passage of a much less progressive tax system—one relying more heavily on consumption taxes and taxation of middle-class incomes—in cooperation with Republicans and a minority of conservative Democrats. They were confident in their ability to administer such broad-based taxes effectively. But they regarded mass-based taxation as a betrayal of the principles of their party. After all, the Democratic Party had strong traditions of representing the disadvantaged, of hostility to a strong central government as the instrument of special privilege, of opposition to the taxation of consumption, and of support for policies designed to widen access to economic opportunity. A failure to adopt a highly progressive and "reconstructive" tax program would have had serious consequences for Wilson and McAdoo. They would have bitterly divided their party. They would have spoiled their opportunities for attracting Republican progressives to their party. And they would have destroyed their strong partnership with

---

[5] Wilson, however, had far greater suspicion of the administrative state than did McAdoo. In 1916, because of that suspicion, Wilson may well have been attracted to using taxation, rather than administrative regulation, to tackle the "monopoly problem." As the war wore on, and as he was unable to resist the growing influence of business within the wartime bureaucracy, Wilson became even more attracted to the anti-monopoly potential of excess-profits taxation. But no scholar has fully explored the linkages between Wilson's approach to the taxation of business and his overall relations with business. Consequently, the issue of whether or not Woodrow Wilson's ideas and policies, considered comprehensively, represent democratic statism or corporate liberalism lies beyond the scope of this book. The best study of Wilson and business during the war is Robert D. Cuff, *The War Industries Board: Business-Government Relations during World War I* (Baltimore: Johns Hopkins University Press, 1973).

congressional Democrats—a partnership that both leaders regarded as necessary for the effective advancement of national administration.[6]

Closely related to the Wilson administration's tax program was its sale of war bonds to middle-class Americans. Rather than tax middle-class Americans at high levels, the Wilson administration employed a voluntary program to mobilize their savings, a strategy that McAdoo called "capitalizing patriotism." He attempted to persuade Americans to change their economic behavior: to reduce consumption, increase savings, and become creditors of the state. He hoped that after the conclusion of the war the middle-class bondholders would be repaid by tax dollars raised from corporations and the wealthiest Americans. He intended to adopt the opposite, from a distributional standpoint, of the kind of debt retirement that had followed the Civil War.

Selling the high-priced bonds directly to average Americans on a multibillion-dollar scale required marketing campaigns far greater in scope than those used anywhere else in the world. Largely through trial and error, the Wilson administration pioneered a vast array of state-controlled national marketing techniques, including the sophisticated analysis of national income and savings. Financing by the new Federal Reserve system, which McAdoo turned into an arm of the Treasury, was important, but not as much as McAdoo's efforts to shift private savings into bonds. In the course of managing and promoting four "Liberty Loans," Secretary McAdoo and the Treasury expanded the federal government's and the nation's knowledge of the social characteristics of capital markets. The Treasury team used information gath-

[6] For a discussion of the sustained hostility toward special privilege within the Democratic Party, see Robert E. Kelley, *The Transatlantic Persuasion: The Liberal-Democratic Mind in the Age of Gladstone* (New York: Alfred A. Knopf, 1969).

ered by its own systematic investigations; it armed itself with modern techniques of mass communication; and it placed its loans deep in the middle class—far deeper than it had during the Civil War or than European governments did in World War I. In the third Liberty Loan campaign (conducted in April 1918), at least one-half of all American families subscribed. Thus, the new public-finance regime installed by the Wilson administration encompassed a revolution in borrowing strategy as well as tax policy.

The Wilson administration also tried to keep middle-class taxes down while guaranteeing business access to capital by adopting a statist or administrative approach to converting capital to the conduct of the war. Benjamin Strong, the governor of the New York Federal Reserve Bank, described the choice confronting the Treasury as a choice between "one school believing that economy could and should be enforced and inflation avoided through establishing higher [interest] rate levels" and "the other school" believing "that economy must be enforced through some system of rationing, or by consumption taxes, or by other methods more scientific, direct, and equitable than high-interest rates." The Treasury's plan relied on the latter approach: to borrow capital at low rates and then develop new government machinery that would guarantee American business adequate access to capital into the postwar period.

As part of this policy element, Secretary McAdoo led an effort to gain control of the nation's capital markets. Beginning in late 1917, when he became concerned about the difficulties that the railroads and other utilities were having in financing wartime expansion, McAdoo led in devising proposals for centralized control that resulted in the formation of the Capital Issues Committee of the Federal Reserve Board, the creation of the War Finance Corporation, the federal takeover of the nation's railroad system, and McAdoo's appointment as director general of the railroads. Outside the Treasury, he pressed Wilson, other members of the

Cabinet, and Congress to increase the federal government's control over prices and the allocation of capital, and to coordinate
and centralize all wartime powers through instruments even more
powerful than the War Industries Board.

The new public finance regime had broad and significant administrative implications. The complex and ambitious program of
taxing and borrowing required a vast expansion of the Treasury's
administrative capacity. A major arm of the Treasury was the
Bureau of Internal Revenue (BIR), whose personnel increased from
4,000 to 15,800 between 1913 and 1920 and which underwent a
reorganization along multifunctional lines, with clear specifica-
tions of responsibilities and chains of command. One of the most
demanding chores of the bureau was the administration of the
excess-profits tax. In the process of interpreting, selling, explaining, and assessing the new business tax, the Treasury created
a modern staff of experts—accountants, lawyers, and economists.
Much of this bureaucracy also implemented the new individual
income tax by processing the huge volume of information on
individual taxpayers. This flow of information resulted from an
"information at the source" provision in the Revenue Act of 1916,
which required corporations to report on salaries, dividends, and
interest payments. In short, the Treasury built a class of media-
tors—defining themselves as experts—whose task was to reconcile
the goals of the corporation and affluent individuals with the
needs of the state. But under McAdoo's leadership, the Treasury
undertook far more than a "broker-state" balancing of contesting
interest groups; it enhanced the power of the state to advance
economic justice and the war.

McAdoo assembled an exceptionally capable team to manage
the Treasury. The team employed "businesslike" methods and
demonstrated intellectual flexibility and entrepreneurship. Lacking
an adequate civil service, McAdoo fashioned within the Treasury
the kind of organization one political scientist has called an "infor-

mal political technocracy," or a "loose grouping of people where
the lines of policy, politics, and administration merge in a complex
jumble of bodies." It was an early example of what would become
a typical expression of America's unique form of a "higher civil
service."[7] For example, within this new bureaucracy, Assistant
Secretary Russell C. Leffingwell supervised all aspects of Treasury
operations, negotiated with Congress, and, as a former partner
and bond specialist in the New York law firm of Cravath &
Henderson, forged connections with the most powerful elements
of the business community as well as with Benjamin Strong and
the Federal Reserve Board. Daniel C. Roper, who served as commissioner of the BIR, was a seasoned federal bureaucrat with
friends in many agencies, and an influential figure in the national
Democratic Party. Crucial in assisting Leffingwell and Roper was
Yale University economist Thomas S. Adams, who served as principal tax adviser and who led in drafting legislation, tying together
the administering of old laws and the formulating of new ones.
John Skelton Williams, comptroller of the currency, helped maintain McAdoo's ties with more radical antibusiness progressives
and made McAdoo seem, by contrast, conservative and reasonable
to many business leaders.

The Treasury group did far more than administer new taxing
and borrowing programs. It served as the Wilson administration's
primary instrument for learning about financial policy and its
social implications, for shaping the definition of financial issues
and administration programs, and for mobilizing support for those
programs. The Treasury group developed a significant degree of
autonomy. It became the means for McAdoo to form and dominate networks linking together competing centers of power within

<hr />

[7] See Hugh Heclo, "The State and America's Higher Civil Service," paper
delivered at Woodrow Wilson Center Conference on the Role of the State
in Recent American History, October 23–24, 1982.

the federal government and linking the government with civil society. Because McAdoo had formed such a group, he was able to design and implement a financial policy with clear social objectives. Under his leadership, the Treasury avoided falling under the control of competing centers of power within the government and of other groups outside. The Treasury escaped the disarray that befell much of the Wilson administration's mobilization effort.

Wilsonian democratic statism finally succumbed to a business counterattack. In 1918, corporate leaders and Republicans found an opening when President Wilson tried to make a case for doubling taxes. Using vigorous antitax, antigovernment campaigns throughout the nation, and anti-Southern campaigns in the West, Republicans gained control of Congress. Then, in 1920, they rode to a presidential victory during the postwar economic depression. The Democratic Party of Woodrow Wilson had failed to do what the Republican Party of Abraham Lincoln had done—establish long-term control of the federal government and create a new party system.

Although defeated politically, the Wilson administration had proved that the American state, despite its weakness, was capable of fighting a sustained, capital-intensive war. The key was popular support. Critically important both to building popular support and to mobilizing resources on a vast scale was the method of finance: progressive taxation and the sale of "the war for democracy" to the American people through bond drives. Both instruments proved to be critical steps in increasing political authority for the federal government—in increasing its ability, through democratic politics, to acquire resources for national defense and the waging of war. The shaping influence of democratic values on mobilization explained the federal government's success in adopting coercive and statist means for financing the war.

The freewheeling debate over federal tax options continued

during the postwar period. Because the federal government had now acquired substantial experience in creating a modern income-tax system, and because tax experts had become more influential within the federal government, the scope of the debate widened. It encompassed not only the reform of income taxation but also the adoption of a variety of new taxes: sophisticated general sales taxes (including a value-added tax), expenditure taxation, undistributed-profits taxation, and federal regulatory taxes.[8]

The Republicans who assumed control of both the presidency and the Congress in 1921 approached tax reform as a means to roll back Wilsonian democratic statism. The three Republican administrations, under the financial leadership of Secretary of the Treasury Andrew Mellon, adopted the basic strategy of protecting capital markets by reducing taxation. But the Republican administrations did not simply roll back expenditures and wartime tax programs. They reduced taxes according to two potentially contradictory goals: responding positively to the demands of powerful new segments of the economy and mediating class conflict.

In reducing taxes, the Republicans attacked the most redistributional parts of the wartime tax system. In the process, they granted substantial tax reductions to corporations and the wealthiest individuals. In 1921 they abolished the excess-profits tax, dashing Claude Kitchin's hopes that the tax would become permanent. In addition, they made the nominal rate structure of the income tax less progressive so that it would be less burdensome on the wealthy. A secondary objective in reducing marginal tax rates in the top brackets was to diminish the incentive for wealthy taxpayers to invest in tax-exempt government bonds. The market for these bonds had grown spectacularly during World War I, and the

---

[8] On the history of federal regulatory taxation, narrowly defined, see Lee, *History of Regulatory Taxation*.

Republicans worried that the tax-exempt bonds drew investment away from other securities.[9]

Also in 1921, in response to intense lobbying, Republicans began to install a wide range of special tax exemptions and deductions, which the highly progressive rate structure of the income tax had made extremely valuable to wealthy taxpayers. The Revenue Acts during the 1920s introduced the preferential taxation of capital gains and a variety of deductions that favored particular industries, deductions such as oil- and gas-depletion allowances.[10]

Along with the new tax structure came enhanced power for the tax-writing committees of Congress. Legislators on these committees discovered how much influence they wielded through the incremental, relatively invisible consideration of valuable loopholes. Although they did not use the term, the legislators had discovered the political appeal of "tax expenditures." They were able to promote what amounted to new expenditure programs by creating pockets of privilege within the tax code. In turn, they won

[9] Mellon also proposed a constitutional amendment removing the tax deductibility of government securities. On the secondary objective of closing this loophole, see Gene Smiley and Richard H. Keehn, "Federal Personal Income Policy in the 1920s," *Journal of Economic History* 55 (June 1995): 285–303. Smiley and Keehn exaggerate the importance of this objective in motivating the Republican program of tax reductions, but they provide some evidence that lowering marginal rates at the top did, in fact, reduce tax avoidance through the purchase of tax-exempt securities.

[10] A "capitalist state" theorist, Ronald King, stresses the importance, and sincerity, of the progrowth arguments of the Republicans who introduced these measures. King argues that Mellon invoked a "hegemonic tax logic" that was finally victorious in the Kennedy-Johnson tax cuts of 1964. See Ronald Frederick King, "From Redistributive to Hegemonic Logic: The Transformation of American Tax Politics, 1894–1963," *Politics and Society* 12 (No. 1, 1983): 1–52. Also on the 1920s, see King's *Money, Time and Politics: Investment Tax Subsidies and American Democracy* (New Haven: Yale University Press, 1993), 104–11.

or maintained the support of powerful groups and individuals while avoiding the political costs associated with raising taxes.

To exert and reinforce their new power, the committees won approval in the Revenue Act of 1926 for creating the Joint Committee on Internal Revenue Taxation (JCIRT), which would become the Joint Committee on Taxation in 1976. Congress originally charged the JCIRT with investigating avenues to simplify the law and with improving its administration, and the professional staff of the JCIRT did increase the technical capabilities of the tax-writing committees. But the JCIRT immediately became primarily a vehicle for enhancing the influence of the senior members of the tax-writing committees.[11]

Secretary Mellon made his greatest impact on the reformed tax system by leading a struggle within the Republican Party to protect income taxation from those who wanted to replace it with a national sales tax. Mellon helped persuade corporations and the wealthiest individuals to accept *some* progressive income taxation and the principle of "ability to pay." This approach would, Mellon told them, demonstrate their civic responsibility and defuse radical attacks on capital. Thus, while shrinking the state, the Republican leadership took care to preserve the progressive income tax, including the corporation income tax, and thereby maintain a revenue system that appeared to promote social justice as well as finance both normal expenditures and tax expenditures. Mellon went so far as to advocate providing a greater reduction in taxes on "earned" than on "unearned" income, and the Revenue Act of 1924 included such a provision. "The fairness of taxing

---

[11] On the formation of the JCIRT see Blakey and Blakey, *The Federal Income Tax*, 542–3 and 546–8. See also Donald R. Kennon and Rebecca M. Rogers, *The Committee on Ways and Means: A Bicentennial History, 1789–1989* (Washington, D.C.: U.S. Government Printing Office, 1989), 330–3, and Thomas J. Reese, *The Politics of Taxation* (Westport, Conn.: Quorum, 1980), 61–88.

more lightly incomes from wages, salaries, or from investments is beyond question," Mellon asserted. He explained, "In the first case, the income is uncertain and limited in duration; sickness or death destroys it and old age diminishes it; in the other, the source of income continues; the income may be disposed of during a man's life and it descends to his heirs."[12] Mellon's strategy was what might be described as the pursuit of enlightened self-interest—as corporate liberalism, in contrast with Wilson's democratic statism. Mellon received crucial support for his approach from the tax-writing committees of Congress. They wanted to preserve the influence they found they could exert under a progressive system of income taxation.

The new program consolidated the flow of income-tax revenues into the Treasury. The portion of general revenues provided to the federal government by indirect taxes (largely the tariff) fell from almost 75 percent in 1902 to about 25 percent in the 1920s; meanwhile, income-tax revenues increased, accounting for nearly 50 percent of the general revenues of the federal government. As in World War I, the income-tax revenues proved to be more abundant than the Treasury experts had forecast, and the Republican administrations enjoyed substantial, growing budget surpluses until the onset of the Great Depression.

The large revenues from income taxation provided the basis for the expansion of federal domestic programs and for the political reinforcement of the World War I tax system. During the 1920s, the federal government expanded its programs of grants-in-aid, which it had begun in 1914 with the support of the Smith-Lever Act for agricultural extension. This grant system provided federal funding that included matching requirements, formulas for distribution among the states, and monitoring of states' expenditure plans. Highway programs were the major beneficiaries; as early as

---

[12] Andrew W. Mellon, *Taxation: The People's Business* (New York: Macmillan, 1924), 56–7.

1921, roughly 40 percent of all highway funding came from the federal government, based on the Federal Aid Road Act of 1916.

Just as had been the case after the Civil War, state and local governments welcomed this new federal funding. The federal revenues helped state and local governments satisfy demands for public services, especially schools and roads, and relieve pressure on their tax systems. State governments became the most swiftly growing level of government during the 1920s, and they replaced their crumbling systems of state property taxation with new arrays of sales taxes (such as gasoline taxes), user charges (such as motor-vehicle fees), and special taxes on corporations and incomes. In 1902, states were getting about 53 percent of their tax revenues from property taxation; by 1927, they raised only about 23 percent from that source. Of the new taxes, those on sales, especially on gasoline, were the most dynamic. Sales taxes increased as a share of state tax revenues from 18 percent in 1902 and 1913 to 27 percent in 1927 and to 38 percent in 1932.

Mellon also strengthened the World War I tax system by protecting and rationalizing the influence of the Treasury. Most important, Mellon promoted the passage of the Budget and Accounting Act of 1921, which drew on the 1911 reports of the Taft Commission to create the first national budget system. The act established presidential responsibility for preparing a comprehensive budget rather than simply assembling and transmitting departmental requests. It created two important agencies: the Bureau of the Budget (located inside the Treasury) to assist in budget preparation, and the General Accounting Office (as an arm of Congress) to conduct independent audits of the federal government.[13]

---

[13] On the movement to establish a national budget system, see Charles Stewart III, *Budget Reform Politics: The Design of the Appropriations Process in the House of Representatives, 1865–1921* (Cambridge: Cambridge University Press, 1989), especially 172–215. On the implementa-

Mellon also attempted to strengthen the Treasury by transforming it into a "nonpartisan" agency. In his book of 1924, *Taxation: The People's Business* (written largely by his expert assistant secretaries), Mellon explained, "tax revision should never be made the football either of partisan or class politics but should be worked out by those who have made a careful study of the subject in its larger aspects and are prepared to recommend the course which, in the end, will prove for the country's best interest."[14]

Mellon was interested in more than scientific policymaking. His main goal was to insulate the Treasury from pressure from Democratic Congresses. He wanted to ensure that the Treasury worked within conservative assumptions about the state and corporate power and within a political framework that advanced the Republican Party. Consequently, when Mellon approached tax cutting during the postwar reconversion and downsizing of government, he rejected the advice of Thomas S. Adams, whom the Mellon Treasury had kept on as its primary tax adviser. If the federal government was to dismantle its wartime system of taxation, Adams believed, it should take the opportunity to replace the system with an economically efficient income tax or a progressive spendings tax, one that would tax "unnecessary or surplus consumption." Adams began to despair of income taxation, concluding that it contained "incurable inequalities and inconsistencies" and had "reached a condition of inequality the gravity of which could scarcely be exaggerated." He advocated eliminating the excess-profits tax and reducing the rate of progression, but he urged avoiding the kind of special deductions introduced by Mel-

tion of the system, see Annette E. Meyer, *Evolution of United States Budgeting: Changing Fiscal and Financial Concepts* (New York: Greenwood Press, 1989).

[14] Mellon, *Taxation: The People's Business*, 10–11.

lon. In addition, Adams favored the integration of corporate and individual income taxation. Rather than follow Adams's lead, Mellon chose to recommend tax cutting that created privileged groups and industries while providing protection to Republican administrations and Congresses against the charge that they favored the abolition of progressive taxation.[15]

The Republican administrations and Congresses of the 1920s had shifted ground within the World War I tax regime. Soak-the-rich remained, but with progressiveness reduced, major loopholes added, and its sharp anticorporate edge dulled. As a consequence of the path-dependent nature of the development of the tax regime initiated by American involvement in World War I, the income tax conveyed very mixed messages about the nature of wealth and civic responsibility in America. Without the wartime crisis, the growth of the federal government almost certainly would have been slower and reliant on some combination of tariff revenues, sales taxes, and low-rate taxation of personal and corporate incomes or spending. That system might have been as riddled with inconsistencies, departures from horizontal equity, and theoretical confusion as the highly progressive tax system that emerged during and after the World War I crisis. But, in contrast to the system that probably would have emerged from a more incremental process, the system for financing World War I involved a substantial raising of the stakes of conflict over tax policy. Along with highly progressive taxation came opportunities both for undertaking massive assaults on wealth and corporate power and for carving out lucrative enclaves of special privilege within the tax code. These high stakes helped keep taxation at the center stage of politics through World War II.

---

[15] For a discussion of Adams's analysis, see Brownlee, "Economists and the Formation of the Modern Tax System," 430–1.

THE GREAT DEPRESSION AND
THE NEW DEAL TAX REGIME

The Great Depression—the nation's worst economic collapse—produced yet another tax regime. Until 1935, however, Depression-driven changes in tax policy were ad hoc quests for short-term economic stimulation and revenue growth rather than efforts to seek comprehensive tax reform. Until then, both the Republican administration of Herbert Hoover and the Democratic administration of Franklin Roosevelt put economic recovery and budgetary considerations ahead of any other concerns while making fiscal policy. Both administrations stressed the need for tax policies that would maintain the confidence of the business community.

In the first phase of its fiscal policy, the Hoover administration, working with Congress, extended the scope of corporate liberalism to include fiscal activism. Judged by the standards of the day, Hoover was an activist in the manipulation of tax rates to stimulate investment and reduce unemployment. Hoover began his innovative program soon after the stock-market crash in 1929. He managed to cut taxes payable in 1930, called on state and local governments (and public utilities as well) to increase capital outlays, and during 1930 and the first half of 1931 pushed up the federal public-works budget, financing projects such as the building of Boulder Dam (begun in 1928 and completed in 1936). As a result of Hoover's policy and supportive congressional action, federal fiscal policy took a distinctly expansive turn between 1929 and 1931. Even if the economy had been in full employment in 1931, and thus had retained a large base for income taxation, the budgetary surplus of $1 billion in 1929 would have become a large deficit—roughly $3 billion by 1931. (This figure is known as the "full-employment deficit," or the revenue deficit that would have been attained had the economy been operating at full employment.) Not until 1936 was the full-employment deficit as large, and not until World War II was the rate of change in the deficit as substantial in an expansionary direction.[16]

In October 1931, however, the Federal Reserve system produced a monetary contraction that severely limited the ability of the nation's banking system to meet domestic demands for currency and credit. Hoover feared that continued deficit spending would increase competition between government and private borrowers, raise long-term interest rates, and inhibit private investment. He also believed that wavering confidence in the dollar within foreign quarters stemmed in part from the persistent deficits of his administration. Reducing the deficits, he was convinced, would diminish the gold flow and thus relieve international pressure on the Federal Reserve Board to tighten the monetary screws. Consequently, in December 1931 Hoover invoked a new phase of his fiscal policy—the phase that has tended to predominate in the public's memory. He asked Congress for tax increases that promised to raise revenues by one-third, and he and his new secretary of the Treasury, Ogden Mills, suggested enacting a general sales tax.[17]

---

[16] The purpose of using the full-employment deficit as a measure of federal fiscal policy is to eliminate the effects on the federal deficit of variations in national income. These variations cause the tax base to rise or fall independently of variations in rates of taxation and obscure the intention of fiscal policy. Thus, even if the federal government did nothing in the face of a depression—that is to say, if the federal government did not change its tax and spending policies—the increase in the deficit that resulted from a declining tax base would suggest that the government had adopted a counter-cyclical fiscal policy. For the full-employment deficit (surplus) data, see E. Cary Brown, "Fiscal Policy in the Thirties: A Reappraisal," *American Economic Review* 46 (December 1956): 857–79.

[17] The best description of the development of Hoover's fiscal policy is Herbert Stein, *The Fiscal Revolution in America* (Chicago: University of Chicago Press, 1969), 6–38. See also William J. Barber, *From New Era to*

The severity of the Depression and the unpopularity of deficits led many congressional Democrats, including Speaker of the House John Nance Garner and all but one of the members of the Ways and Means Committee, to support a general sales tax. But a group of Democratic insurgents in the House, led by Robert L. Doughton of North Carolina (the only member of the Ways and Means Committee to oppose the sales tax), and Fiorello La Guardia of New York, challenged the House leadership. Doughton described the tax as a violation of "ability to pay" and as a measure that would undercut the plans of some state governments to enact general sales taxes. He and the insurgents worried that the general sales tax might replace the income tax as the centerpiece of the federal tax system, just as Garner's patron, the publisher William Randolph Hearst, intended. The insurgents won the support of most House Democrats and blocked the general sales tax. Doughton privately described the victory as "the greatest victory . . . achieved for the common people since the days of Woodrow Wilson."

In the end, the Revenue Act of 1932, enacted with bipartisan support, did impose some new federal sales taxes (on gasoline, electricity, refrigerators, and telephone messages, for example) but increased revenues mainly by raising personal and corporate income-tax rates across the board and by reducing income-tax exemptions. The act imposed the largest peacetime tax increases in the nation's history.

Taxation was not a central issue in the critical election of 1932, but the politics of the Revenue Act of 1932 may have advanced the career of Franklin D. Roosevelt. Speaker Garner's support of

New Deal: Herbert Hoover, the Economists, and American Economic Policy, 1921–1933 (Cambridge: Cambridge University Press, 1985). Both scholars pay close attention to the role of ideas and actors inside the federal government in shaping tax policy.

the general sales tax damaged his candidacy for the Democratic presidential nomination, and almost all of the congressional insurgents backed Roosevelt's candidacy. Voters who were upset over the large tax increases may well have blamed them on Hoover and the Republicans.[18]

In the first 100 days of his administration, Franklin Roosevelt moved beyond the corporate liberalism of Herbert Hoover to apply the coercive power of government to the tasks of relief and economic recovery. It may have been a high-water mark for democratic statism, but not for the implementation of tax principles in the democratic-statist tradition. This was true despite the fact that, like Woodrow Wilson before him, Roosevelt was personally devoted to *both* balanced budgets and redistributional taxation. In the 1932 campaign, Roosevelt pledged to balance the federal budget, which for three years the administration of Herbert Hoover had been unable to do. In 1933, Roosevelt warned Congress, "too often in recent history liberal governments have been wrecked on the rocks of loose fiscal policy." Also, Roosevelt personally opposed general sales taxes, which he regarded as "the last word in foolishness," and favored soak-the-rich taxation—shifting the tax burden to the wealthiest individuals and corporations according to "ability to pay."[19] Moreover, he recognized the large

---

[18] For the quotations from Robert Doughton, and for an excellent description of the congressional consideration of the Revenue Act of 1932, see Walter K. Lambert, "New Deal Revenue Acts: The Politics of Taxation" (Ph.D. dissertation, University of Texas, Austin, 1970), 1–103. See also Jordan A. Schwarz, "John Nance Garner and the Sales Tax Rebellion of 1932," *Journal of Southern History* 30 (May 1964): 162–80.

[19] In 1932, after his election, Roosevelt outlined his views on sales taxation through a letter from Felix Frankfurter to Walter Lippmann. See Max Freedman, ed., *Roosevelt and Frankfurter: Their Correspondence, 1928–1945* (Boston: Little, Brown, 1967), 68. On Roosevelt's opposition to sales taxation in the transition of 1932–33, see Frank Freidel, *Franklin D. Roosevelt: Launching the New Deal* (Boston: Little, Brown, 1973), 53.

constituency that the Depression had created for the sort of tax reform—redistributional and anticorporate—undertaken by the Wilson administration. Nonetheless, in contrast with the early phase of Wilson's financing of World War I, Roosevelt's early New Deal brought no progressive fiscal innovations.[20]

Depression conditions posed massive problems for Roosevelt, problems that Wilson had not faced in the expansive years of 1916 and 1917. The problems were political and economic. The fact that the Great Depression had shrunk the tax base meant that a serious effort at pay-as-you-go financing of expensive New Deal programs would have required massive increases in tax rates or the introduction of substantial new taxes. Both Roosevelt and Congress disliked having to pick the losers in the political game of increasing taxes. Both feared, in particular, that a democratic-statist tax policy would arouse business opposition to innovative New Deal programs and pave the way for a conservative counter-attack on the New Deal if economic recovery failed. On this score they had learned from Wilson's experience. Roosevelt, the Democratic candidate for vice president in 1920, remembered all too well the success of the Republican backlash against Wilsonian taxation during the economic troubles of 1918–20. Worrisome too—though of less consequence to Roosevelt and Congress—were the possible economic effects of democratic-statist taxation.

---

[20] A very different view of Roosevelt and his program can be found in the work of historian Mark Leff, who argues that Franklin D. Roosevelt looked only for symbolic victories in tax reform. See Mark H. Leff, *The Limits of Symbolic Reform: The New Deal and Taxation* (Cambridge: Cambridge University Press, 1984). Walter Lambert found no evidence that Roosevelt favored a radical distribution of tax burdens, but he did find a deep ethical commitment to the principle of "ability to pay." See Lambert, "New Deal Revenue Acts," passim. See also W. Elliot Brownlee, "Taxation as an X-ray," *Reviews in American History* 14 (March 1986): 121–6.

They acknowledged that if they raised income and corporate taxes sufficiently to balance the budget in the short run, they might run the risk of worsening the economic depression by undermining business confidence and investment.

Finally, Roosevelt faced an important institutional barrier to a democratic-statist tax policy. Twelve years of Republican leadership had built a Treasury staff that was unenthusiastic about undertaking the work of devising new progressive taxes. Roosevelt's long-term secretary of the Treasury, Henry Morgenthau, Jr., did not take office until January 1934, and his immediate deputies needed several years to rebuild a capability within the department for advancing democratic-statist reform. Meanwhile, Roosevelt instructed him to leave the proposal of new taxes to Congress and, in particular, to the Ways and Means Committee, now under Doughton's leadership.

During the first two years of the New Deal, the combination of Roosevelt's hostility to sales taxation and progressive initiatives on the part of Congress produced the adoption of modest increases in income taxes and loophole-closing reforms. The National Industrial Recovery Act imposed a 5 percent tax on dividends and a small excess-profits tax; it also tightened provisions for deducting business and capital losses. The Agricultural Adjustment Act added a tax on food processing. In addition, other acts restored the earned-income credit, slightly increased the progressiveness of income-tax rates, and raised capital-gains taxes.[21]

But during these years Congress and the Roosevelt administration relied less heavily on tax increases than on automatic revenue increases that resulted from the interaction of existing taxes (enhanced by the Hoover administration's Revenue Act of 1932) and from the economic recovery that began in 1933. The repeal of

---

[21] On the importance of the sales-tax issue during the first year of the New Deal, see Freidel, *Franklin D. Roosevelt,* 51–9 and 446–51.

Prohibition was especially timely. Liquor taxes were still on the books and were far more popular among Democratic voters than general sales taxes or other excises. Between 1933 and 1936, revenues from alcohol taxes increased by almost $500 million. In 1936, special excise taxes, led by the increases in liquor taxes and levies on tobacco and gasoline consumption, produced about $1.5 billion, which was more than 40 percent of federal tax collections and larger than the $1.4 billion raised by income taxes in that year. (In 1936 only about 2 million American households—out of a total of 32 million—owed any federal income tax; the personal income tax accounted for less than half of income-tax collections.) In addition, Roosevelt and Congress allowed federal deficits to grow—from $2.6 billion in 1933 to $4.4 billion in 1936, more than 40 percent of federal expenditures. During his first term, in every annual budget message Roosevelt asserted that the deficits would disappear along with the Depression.[22]

In 1935 Roosevelt decided that political and economic conditions favored a resumption of a democratic-statist tax policy. Most important, the growing "Thunder on the Left," particularly Huey Long's "Share Our Wealth" movement, opened the way for vigorous redistributional taxation designed to remedy flaws in the nation's economic structure. Moreover, Roosevelt had gained confidence in the prospects for economic recovery and was less worried about a business backlash. And Morgenthau had finally established the required infrastructure of professional expertise within the Treasury.[23]

---

[22] For an analysis of the trends of the various federal revenue sources during the Great Depression, see John M. Firestone, *Federal Receipts and Expenditures during Business Cycles, 1879–1958* (Princeton: Princeton University Press, 1960), 36–54.

[23] The following account of the making of tax policy within the Roosevelt administration through World War II draws on John Morton Blum, *From the Morgenthau Diaries: Years of Crisis, 1928–1938* (Boston: Houghton

Morgenthau's staff contained a group of law professors, including General Counsel Herman Oliphant and Roswell Magill. Magill, a tax expert from Columbia University, directed a comprehensive survey of the federal tax system in preparation for a reform initiative. The monetary economist Jacob Viner also advised Morgenthau on tax issues, and Carl S. Shoup, Roy Blough, and Lawrence H. Seltzer—all economists who specialized in public finance—worked closely with Magill. Central to their work was an intensified effort to study the distributional effects of taxation at all levels of government.[24]

At the end of the summer of 1934, Magill and his colleagues in the Treasury had presented Morgenthau with recommendations designed to raise new revenues and attack concentrations of wealth; in December, Morgenthau had forwarded the proposals to the White House. In developing a tax proposal for Congress, Roosevelt drew assistance from his close adviser Felix Frankfurter.

Mifflin, 1959), 297–337 and 439–51; *From the Morgenthau Diaries: Years of Urgency, 1938–1941* (Boston: Houghton Mifflin, 1965), 22–30 and 278–318; and *From the Morgenthau Diaries: Years of War, 1941– 1945* (Boston: Houghton Mifflin, 1967), 33–78. Blum's still stands as the best general treatment of this subject. Also valuable is Randolph Paul, *Taxation in the United States* (Boston: Little, Brown, 1954), 168–406. See as well Lambert, "New Deal Revenue Acts," for excellent details on the relationship between the Roosevelt administration and Congress.

[24] The most important study of tax incidence undertaken during the 1930s was the unpublished analysis of economist Louis Shere. See "The Burden of Taxation," unpublished memorandum, U.S. Department of the Treasury, Division of Research and Taxation, 1934. For an excellent survey of the modern measurement of tax burden in the United States, see B. K. Atrostic and James R. Nunns, "Measuring Tax Burden: A Historical Perspective," in Ernest R. Berndt and Jack E. Triplett, eds., *Fifty Years of Economic Measurement: The Jubilee of the Conference on Research in Income and Wealth, National Bureau of Economic Research Studies in Income and Wealth,* Volume 54 (Chicago: University of Chicago Press, 1990), 343–408.

From the outset of the New Deal, he had been urging the president to use the taxing power to attack bigness in business. Roosevelt and Frankfurter used the Treasury recommendations to craft an ambitious program of radical tax reform, which Roosevelt presented to Congress in June. Roosevelt told Secretary of the Interior Harold Ickes that the speech was "the best thing he had done as President."[25]

Roosevelt proposed a graduated tax on corporations to check the growth of monopoly, a tax on the dividends that holding companies received from corporations they controlled, surtaxes to raise the maximum income-tax rate on individuals from 63 to 79 percent, and an inheritance tax, to be imposed in addition to federal estate taxation. In his message to Congress, he explained that accumulations of wealth meant "great and undesirable concentration of control in relatively few individuals over the employment and welfare of many, many others." Moreover, "whether it be wealth achieved through the cooperation of the entire community or riches gained by speculation—in either case the ownership of such wealth or riches represents a great public interest and a great ability to pay." But Roosevelt's goal was not a simplistic redistribution of wealth and power. Later that year, he explained to a newspaper publisher that his purpose was "not to destroy wealth, but to create a broader range of opportunity, to restrain the growth of unwholesome and sterile accumulations and to lay the burdens of Government where they can best be carried." Thus,

---

[25] On the significance of Frankfurter's interest in this tax legislation, see Ellis Hawley, *The New Deal and the Problem of Monopoly: Study in Economic Ambivalence* (Princeton: Princeton University Press, 1966), 344–59. Hawley, however, concludes that the Revenue Acts of 1935 and 1936 were "relatively innocuous" (359). Harold Ickes's discussion of the 1935 tax measure is in the June 19, 1935, entry in his diaries, in the Harold L. Ickes Papers, Library of Congress.

he justified his tax-reform program in terms of both its inherent equity and its ability to liberate the energies of individuals and small corporations, thereby advancing recovery.[26]

In the Revenue Act of 1935, Congress gave Roosevelt much of the tax reform he wanted. In that year, and throughout the peace-time New Deal, Roosevelt was able to count on the support of Doughton, who served as chair of the House Ways and Means Committee from 1933 until 1947. (Counting a second term, from 1949 to 1953, he was the longest serving chair of the committee in its history.) Doughton's support was often decisive in Congress, where Senator Pat Harrison of Mississippi, chair of the Senate Finance Committee, and other conservative southern Democrats often opposed New Deal tax reform. Doughton at times had his doubts about the more sophisticated New Deal tax proposals and resisted large tax increases of any kind. He privately complained in 1935, "we have had too many theories in key places under this administration." But he believed in the justice of shifting the distribution of taxes away from the "poor, weak, and humble," who—he was certain—paid a higher percentage of their incomes in taxes than did the wealthy. And, ever since he had begun his service in Congress in 1911, he had put party loyalty and the need to establish a record of Democratic leadership first.[27]

Offsetting the progressiveness of Roosevelt's income-tax re-

[26] For the Roosevelt quotations, see Arthur M. Schlesinger, Jr., *The Age of Roosevelt: The Politics of Upheaval* (Boston: Houghton Mifflin, 1960), 328, and Lambert, "New Deal Revenue Acts," 259–60.

[27] For suggestions as to the significance to the early New Deal of Doughton in particular and southern congressmen in general, see Tindall, *Emergence of the New South*, 607–13. Pat Harrison was less energetic and effective than Doughton, but he was able to kill Roosevelt's proposal for the taxation of inheritances in 1935. The Doughton quotations are from Lambert, "New Deal Revenue Acts," 297 and 226.

forms was the regressiveness of the payroll taxes that were enacted in 1935 as a central part of the Social Security system.[28] The incongruity might suggest that Roosevelt was little more than a cynical manipulator of the powerful symbolism of taxation. But Roosevelt conceived of Social Security as an insurance system. He thought of the taxes paid by middle-class people as premiums that established investments. Thus, in his mind, taxpayers received the benefits for which they had paid. Roosevelt's concept was shared by much of the American public, and it lent the payroll tax a popularity that gave it an edge in winning a narrow victory in 1935. Franklin Roosevelt's leadership, including his support of the social-insurance experts who favored funding through payroll taxes, was largely responsible for the victory for old-age insurance.[29]

In addition, Roosevelt realized that the insurance principle worked to protect the system from conservative counterattack. Roosevelt believed, "with those taxes in there, no damn politician can ever scrap my social security program." He succeeded, probably beyond his wildest expectations, in protecting Social Security.

[28] For histories of the adoption of Social Security told from the perspectives of experts within the Roosevelt administration, see Edwin E. Witte, *The Development of the Social Security Act: A Memorandum on the History of the Committee on Economic Security and Drafting and Legislative History of the Social Security Act* (Madison: University of Wisconsin Press, 1963), and Arthur J. Altmeyer, *The Formative Years of Social Security: A Chronicle of Social Security Legislation and Administration, 1934–1954* (Madison: University of Wisconsin Press, 1968). See also Theron F. Schlabach, *Edwin E. Witte: Cautious Reformer* (Madison: University of Wisconsin Press, 1969).

[29] For a history of the financing of Social Security that stresses the importance of Roosevelt's role in 1935, see Edward D. Berkowitz, "Social Security and the Financing of the American State," in W. Elliot Brownlee, ed., *Funding the Modern American State, 1941–1995: The Rise and Fall of the Era of Easy Finance* (Washington, D.C.: Woodrow Wilson Center Press; Cambridge: Cambridge University Press, 1995), 149–94.

In addition, the benefit formula of even the initial Social Security program had a progressive dimension. In 1939, Roosevelt and Congress firmly established a progressive benefit formula and introduced pay-as-you-go financing.[30]

Roosevelt believed that the passage of the Revenue Act of 1935 meant that he would not have to request any further new taxes until after the presidential election of 1936. But in early 1936, the Supreme Court invalidated the processing tax of the Agricultural Adjustment Act, and Congress overrode Roosevelt's veto of a bonus bill for World War I veterans. Both events threatened a substantial increase in the federal deficit.

In response, Morgenthau again recommended an undistributed profits tax, a revenue-raising measure that Roosevelt had previously ignored. The proposal was to eliminate the existing taxes on corporate income, capital stock, and excess profits and replace them with a tax on retained earnings—the profits that corporations did not distribute to their stockholders. The tax would be graduated according to the proportion of the profits that were undistributed. Magill's team of experts had discovered this idea when digging into the Treasury archives for inspiration. They had discovered Thomas S. Adams's 1919 proposal for an undistributed-profits tax, which he had favored as a replacement for excess-profits taxation.[31]

Morgenthau and his Treasury staff held the view that the mea-

---

[30] One historian of the origins of Social Security describes the 1939 changes as designed to "speed up the creation of vested interests in the program, create coalitions of beneficiaries whose interests were coincidental with those of the bureaucracy, and eliminate the potential discipline of a funded system." See Carolyn L. Weaver, *The Crisis in Social Security: Economic and Political Origins* (Durham, N.C.: Duke University Press, 1982), 112.

[31] For evidence of Adams's influence, see Louis Shere, assistant secretary of the Treasury, to Robert M. Haig, March 6, 1936, Robert Murray Haig Papers, Butler Library, Columbia University.

sure would fight both tax avoidance and the concentration of corporate power. Corporations, they were convinced, deliberately retained profits to avoid the taxation of dividends under the individual income tax. Further, they believed that the largest corporations had the power to retain shares of surpluses greater than those retained by small companies. The surpluses, they were certain, gave large corporations an unfair competitive advantage by reducing the need to borrow new capital. Moreover, the Treasury claimed that the tax would promote recovery. Oliphant and Morgenthau believed that large corporations saved excessively or reinvested their surpluses unwisely. The undistributed-profits tax would provide a powerful incentive for such corporations to distribute their profits to their shareholders. Those shareholders, in turn, as Oliphant and Federal Reserve Board chair Marriner Eccles stressed, would spend some portion of their dividends and thus stimulate the economy.

Roosevelt endorsed the undistributed-profits tax in a message to Congress in March and received support, in principle, from the Ways and Means Committee. But the administration faced the hostility of the Senate Finance Committee and its staff, which feared revenue loss and preferred retaining the existing corporate income taxes while adding a small, flat tax on undistributed earnings. In June 1936 Congress passed a graduated tax on undistributed profits, despite heavy business lobbying against Roosevelt's proposal and intense wrangling over widely divergent revenue estimates. Morgenthau intervened in the negotiations between the House and the Senate and had much to do with the outcome. Because of Senate objections, the graduation was less severe than the Treasury had wanted, but Congress kept the corporate income tax besides passing the undistributed-profits tax.

The new corporate tax posed the greatest threat to the autonomy of corporate finance since the passage of the excess-profits tax during World War I. In July, Secretary of the Interior Ickes talked with industrialist Harry F. Guggenheim and concluded, "the fundamental policy issue today is taxation." The increases in the higher brackets, "taxing surpluses in corporation treasuries, and fear of further increases," Ickes wrote, had made "a bitter enemy out of practically everyone" among the "very rich."[32]

Throughout Morgenthau's service as secretary of the Treasury, he sought, with Roosevelt's support, the prosecution of tax evaders and the closing of loopholes used by tax avoiders. Most spectacularly, in 1934 the Treasury promoted the prosecution of its former secretary, Andrew Mellon, for tax evasion. The Treasury claimed Mellon owed more than $3 million in back taxes and penalties. Morgenthau told the government prosecutor, "I consider that Mr. Mellon is not on trial but Democracy and the privileged rich and I want to see who will win." Mellon won in court but lost the public-relations battle. A grand jury refused to indict, and in 1937 the Board of Tax Appeals found him innocent of tax evasion. But the board also said he had made errors that happened to be in his favor and added that he owed $400,000 in back taxes.

The board used the Mellon case to publicize the loopholes in the tax code. The commissioner pointed out that as secretary of the Treasury, Mellon had solicited from the Bureau of Internal Revenue "a memorandum setting forth the various ways by which an individual may legally avoid tax." It turned out that Mellon had used five of the ten methods detailed in the memorandum, as well as some others that he had devised on his own.

In spring 1937, the outcome of the Mellon case, coupled with a $600 million shortfall in tax revenues—a deficit that Treasury analysts blamed on tax avoidance—led Morgenthau and Roosevelt to seek remedial legislation. At the same time that the Treasury systematically investigated tax avoidance, Roosevelt won the

---

[32] See July 27, 1936, entry in the Harold Ickes Diaries, Ickes Papers.

support of the chairs of the tax-writing committees for creating the Joint Committee on Tax Evasion and Avoidance, with power to acquire the names of tax avoiders from the Treasury. With staff assistance from Thurman Arnold, whom the Treasury borrowed from the Department of Justice, Treasury witnesses inventoried loopholes and identified sixty-seven "large, wealthy taxpayers" who had used the device of incorporation to reduce their taxes. The press zeroed in on Alfred P. Sloan, the president of General Motors, who had incorporated his yacht. Sloan explained, "While no one should desire to avoid payment of his share [of taxes,] neither should anyone be expected to pay more than is lawfully required."[33]

The evidence mobilized by the Joint Committee persuaded Congress to pass, unanimously, the Revenue Act of 1937. The measure increased taxation of personal holding companies, limited deductions for corporate yachts and country estates, restricted deductions for losses from sales or exchanges of property, reduced incentives for the creation of multiple trusts, and eliminated favors for nonresident taxpayers. These increases, coupled with those undertaken the year before, raised tax rates high enough to create a full-employment surplus—the revenue surplus that would have been attained had the economy been operating at full employment. (This was the only year in which New Deal fiscal policy created a full-employment surplus, and not a deficit.)

The economic recovery, which had cut the rate of unemployment in half by 1937, encouraged Roosevelt to plan an even more intense reform program in 1938. He intended to increase the undistributed-profits tax, to establish a graduated tax on capital gains, and to tax the income from federal, state, and local bonds.

These ambitious plans, more than any other dimension of the New Deal, aroused fear and hostility on the part of large corpora-

---

[33] Blum, *Morgenthau Diaries: Years of Crisis*, 335.

tions. They correctly viewed Roosevelt's tax program as a threat to their control over capital and their latitude for financial planning. There is no evidence that capital went "on strike," as many New Dealers charged, citing a lag in business investment. But business leaders searched for a political opening. Unfortunately for Roosevelt's tax program, he made major tactical errors: reinforcing the recession of 1937–8 and opening in 1937 the disastrous fight to restructure the Supreme Court. These mistakes provided the opening. Conservative Democrats, led by Bernard Baruch and Joseph P. Kennedy, broke with the president and argued that tax cuts were necessary to restore business confidence. They agreed with Senator Pat Harrison, who declared in December 1937 that Roosevelt's tax program had "retarded progress and contributed to the unemployment situation."[34]

In 1938, a coalition of Republicans and conservative Democrats, working through the tax-writing committees, took advantage of Roosevelt's mistakes to try to block any more New Deal tax reform. Roosevelt fought back, denouncing at a Jackson Day dinner the businessmen "who will fight to the last ditch to retain such autocratic control over the industry and finances of the country as they now possess." But conservative Democrats had gathered enough strength to push through Congress, over the opposition of Ways and Means Chair Robert Doughton, a measure that gutted the tax on undistributed profits and discarded the graduated corporate income tax. Roosevelt, respecting the strength of the opposition, decided not to veto the bill. Instead, he allowed the Revenue Act of 1938 to become law without his signature and denounced it as the "abandonment of an important principle of American taxation"—taxation according to ability to pay. In 1939, Congress wiped out the undistributed-profits tax and formally eradicated the brief episode of radical tax reform.

---

[34] For the Harrison quotation, see Lambert, "New Deal Revenue Acts," 422.

Roosevelt's defeats in 1938 and 1939 also signaled a reassertion of congressional power over the shape of revenue legislation. From that time until the end of World War II, the tax-writing committees of Congress carefully maintained their control over the initiation of tax policy. The influence of Morgenthau and his Treasury advisers had waned; they were able to influence Congress decisively only when Roosevelt was able to mobilize public opinion.

The New Deal program of tax reform ended in the late 1930s, but Roosevelt and Congress had already ushered in a new tax regime, composed of a strengthened soak-the-rich component, an expanded taxation of consumption, and the new Social Security taxes. The Roosevelt administration did not redistribute income through taxation to any great extent, but overall the tax system had become somewhat more progressive. And Roosevelt's program of reform of income taxation had conditioned Americans to expect that significant tax increases would take place through increasing taxes on the wealthy and on corporations. Whatever its redistributional limitations, the new system dramatically enhanced the revenue capacity of the federal government. Despite the fact that in 1941 (fiscal year) economic recovery had not yet restored full employment, federal tax collections—led by Social Security taxes, consumption taxes, and corporate income taxes—had more than doubled; collections had increased from $2.9 billion in 1929 to $7.4 billion in 1941.

The expansion of this federal tax capacity found a welcome audience in state and local governments, just as it had during the post–Civil War era and the 1920s. The early 1930s had been especially traumatic for state and local leaders, and they generally applauded the reduced pressure on their tax systems. Local governments had faced sharply increased relief obligations but suffered declining property-tax revenues, soaring rates of default, and even popular revolts, including a tax strike in Chicago. States had provided growing subventions for local governments by increasing sales taxes and reducing spending on highways and schools. State constitutions, however, limited deficit finance, and new state and municipal bonds were extremely difficult to market. As the Depression worsened in 1931 and 1932, state and local governments found it impossible to conduct business as usual and still balance their budgets. They adopted more drastic economies, scaled back total expenditures in 1931, and sharply contracted spending in 1933 and 1934. State and local governments had pushed up tax rates every year between 1929 and 1933, and they maintained those high levels until 1936, when they raised them even further.

State governments also increased the scope and rates of their sales taxes until, in 1940, they were raising most of their funds through such levies. By 1940, consumer taxes—on gasoline, tobacco, liquor, soft drinks, and oleomargarine—produced $1.1 billion, and the new general retail-sales taxes, which thirty-three states adopted between 1932 and 1937, produced $500 million. Meanwhile, local governments increased their effective rates of property taxation.

In its latter stages, the New Deal did much to strengthen state and local revenue systems through a massive, complex system of intergovernmental transfers, which accounted for more than 10 percent of state and local revenues by the end of the New Deal, and through the promotion of taxpaying. A key example of such promotion was the work of the Home Owners' Loan Corporation (HOLC), which required borrowers to pay off back taxes as a condition for receiving subsidized mortgage loans.[35]

---

[35] Economist John J. Wallis argues that New Deal programs "explain" the relative decline of local governments and the sustained growth of state governments during the 1930s. See Wallis, "The Birth of Old Federalism: Financing the New Deal, 1932–1940," *Journal of Economic History* 44 (March 1984): 139–59. David Beito argues that tactics such as those of the HOLC were part of a larger strategy to undermine traditional, virtuous resistance to taxpaying. See his *Tax Payers in Revolt: Tax Resistance during the Great Depression* (Chapel Hill: University of North Carolina Press, 1989).

The demise of New Deal tax reform was part of a larger collapse of any political effort to develop a comprehensive, democratic-statist program. The New Deal had thrust the federal government into new zones, but the American public had not embraced a coherent theory that would justify the greatly expanded state. Instead, the various groups that the New Deal had served tended, on the one hand, to embrace the capitalist order and, on the other, to appreciate the particular benefits they had received. These groups wanted the rewards of capitalism but expected the federal government to protect them from substantial risks in the marketplace and, when social discord became too severe, to broker agreements with rival entities. Those agreements might involve, for example, favored treatment in the tax code, through special exemptions or deductions, for particular groups. But the agreements did not encompass far-reaching tax reform—reform that could have produced broad shifts in the distribution of taxation.

The Roosevelt administration's innovation of the broker state was associated with an assumption of a greater responsibility for promoting economic recovery through fiscal mechanisms such as cutting taxes, increasing expenditures, or expanding deficits. But this assumption of responsibility was slow, erratic, and by the time of American entry into World War II, highly incomplete.[36]

It is true that, judging by *actual* deficits, the Roosevelt administration's fiscal policy might be interpreted as one of consistent, and increasingly more vigorous, promotion of economic recovery through deficit spending. However, the deficits were often unintentional results of a depressed tax base and were always unwelcome

[36] The following account of the development of Roosevelt's fiscal policy draws from the sources cited previously and from Stein, *Fiscal Revolution in America*, 39–196, which remains the best general treatment of the subject.

to Roosevelt. In fact, only about half of the Roosevelt deficits resulted from deliberate policy decisions. Roosevelt and Morgenthau never intended the deficits to be a permanent feature of the nation's system of public finance.[37]

During Roosevelt's first term, in 1933 and 1935, the president and Congress adopted an expansionary fiscal policy. But the stimulus was only modest. Because of the persistent efforts of Roosevelt and Morgenthau to balance the budget, his first-term fiscal policy was no more expansive than that of Hoover between 1929 and 1931. In fact, Roosevelt's policy was more conservative than Hoover's. In contrast with Hoover, Roosevelt had succeeded in liberating monetary policy from Federal Reserve control and in creating an expansive money supply. Consequently, he did not face Hoover's problem: that increased deficits were likely to drive up interest rates to the point of discouraging borrowing. Roosevelt certainly had not chosen to seek salvation in the prescriptions of John Maynard Keynes, who, in *The Means to Prosperity,* had urged Depression governments to stimulate private investment through the vigorous use of deficits. Recalling a visit with Roosevelt in 1934, Keynes remarked that he had "supposed the president was more literate, economically speaking." Roosevelt remembered that Keynes "left a whole rigmarole of figures." Roosevelt added, "He must be a mathematician rather than a political economist."

In 1938, after both tax reform and economic recovery had faltered, Roosevelt did adopt a more reformist fiscal policy—moving it toward a Keynesian position. Near the end of the recession

---

[37] The stimulus of the deficits pales even further in the light of state and local fiscal policy. State and local governments enacted such large tax increases between 1933 and 1939 that they would have had huge budget surpluses if the economy had been at full employment. The state and local full-employment surpluses were large enough to offset the expansive effects of federal deficits in all but two of those seven years.

of 1937–38, Roosevelt launched an energetic new spending program that was unaccompanied by significant tax increases. Consequently, the full-employment surplus became a full-employment deficit, and it surged upward in 1938 and 1939.

But the influence of Keynesian ideas on Roosevelt's fiscal policy was still only indirect; Roosevelt had not become a convert. He had shifted policy largely because he decided to abandon tax reform. He recognized that conservative opposition to the New Deal had grown too strong for him to seek significant tax increases or to pursue economic recovery through his preferred means, redistributional tax reform. Moreover, Roosevelt could not ignore the strong indications that restrictive fiscal policy had contributed to the sharp downturn in 1937–38. Consequently, he listened more closely to a group of government officials, scattered across the Works Progress Administration, the Department of Agriculture, and the Federal Reserve, who had become more partial to deficits and had begun to discover, in the work of John Maynard Keynes, a rationale for their political position. There is no evidence that Harry Hopkins, Henry Wallace, or Marriner Eccles ever convinced Roosevelt of their view that permanent deficits would be necessary to achieve and maintain full employment. However, Roosevelt did adopt a Keynesian argument to justify his shift in tax policy. In 1938 he explained to Congress that his large increases in expenditures, unaccompanied by tax increases, would add "to the purchasing power of the Nation."

During the years of economic recovery immediately before Pearl Harbor, economists within the federal government intensified the advancement of Keynesian ideas. Some, like Alvin Hansen, were senior economists who learned Keynes's concepts late in their careers but used his ideas to order their long-standing beliefs that economic stagnation was inevitable without permanent deficits or drastic income redistribution. Others were weaned on *The General Theory*, which appeared in 1936. These economists staffed agencies such as the Division of Industrial Economics within the Department of Commerce, the Bureau of the Budget (including the Office of Statistical Standards, created in 1939), and the National Resources Planning Board. Within the Treasury, the economists Harry Dexter White and Lawrence H. Seltzer, chief economist in the Research Division, began to promote and apply Keynesian ideas. All these economists, and their colleagues outside government, had a significant effect on expert advisers throughout the Roosevelt administration. These experts included many of the lawyers who advised Morgenthau within the Treasury. As early as 1937, Magill argued for budget-balancing over a number of years. He explained, "The effects of borrowing will be stimulating to the national economy." Oliphant was even more explicitly Keynesian. And the New York tax lawyer Randolph Paul, who took over the Tax Division in late 1941 and became general counsel in mid-1942, was the most vigorous in pressing Keynesian ideas upon Morgenthau.

But the success of Keynesian ideas was limited at the time of American entry into World War II. Within the Treasury, Morgenthau never abandoned his desire to balance budgets on an annual basis, although he encouraged argument over this point among his expert advisers. Within the administration at large, Keynesian advocates had succeeded in establishing a consensus on only two vague propositions. The first was that the federal government should avoid adopting restrictive fiscal policies (such as the Hoover administration's tax increase of 1932 and Roosevelt's expenditure cuts of 1937) during recession or depression conditions. The second was that the federal government should expand spending programs during economic reversals. But the Roosevelt administration had not translated these ideas into a clearly defined strategy of spending and deficits. The administration had created no federal agency with the responsibility or the capability for specifying reliable techniques and magnitudes.

The Roosevelt administration had, however, taken important steps toward the centralization of budgetary authority. In 1939 the Reorganization Act created the Executive Office of the President (EOP), transferred to it the Bureau of the Budget (from Treasury) and the National Resources Planning Board (from Interior), and established within the EOP the Office of Emergency Management. For public consumption, Congress emphasized the goal of reducing expenditures through coordination and elimination of overlapping agencies, but the primary purpose was to enhance presidential control over a greatly expanded executive branch. Thus, at the same time that the Roosevelt administration edged toward the embrace of deficit spending as a positive good, it moved toward a more self-conscious use of the federal budget as an instrument of national policy.

By the end of the 1930s, democratic statism was played out as the determining force in the development of federal taxation. But the tax regime instituted by Franklin Roosevelt's New Deal was still very much in place, although it had become less ambitious in its redistributional scope than between 1935 and 1938. To President Franklin Roosevelt and some of his advisers, it seemed that intervention in another world war—an intervention managed once again by a Democratic administration—would be the occasion for renewed victories for democratic statism.

3

◦━◦

The era of easy finance, 1941–1986

World War II, like the great national emergencies before it, created opportunities for public-finance reforms that had clear social intent and organizational coherence. As had been the case during World War I and the Great Depression, decisive presidential leadership contributed significantly to the creation of a new tax regime. Motivated by a concern for social justice as well as by the threat to the nation's security, the administration of President Franklin D. Roosevelt shaped the enactment of a wartime tax regime and then exercised initiative in using the media to persuade Americans to accept it. The new regime proved even more resilient after the war than the World War I regime had been during the 1920s. In fact, the World War II tax system has remained at the core of federal finance ever since World War II.

THE FORMATION OF THE TAX REGIME

As Americans prepared for entry into World War II, President Franklin Roosevelt and the congressional leadership assumed that mobilization would be on a much greater scale than during World

War I and that the inflationary pressures would be even more severe. As a consequence, the nation's leadership quickly reached a bipartisan consensus favoring large tax increases. These increases would finance a major portion of the war and, at the same time, control inflation by discouraging consumers from bidding up prices in competition with the government. Therefore, the leaders of both political parties assumed that wartime tax increases would be even larger than during World War I. Despite the consensus, the political process of adopting this new fiscal policy was neither smooth nor direct. The specific taxes and the level of taxation employed turned out to be matters of severe contention.

The war presented Roosevelt with another opportunity to resuscitate democratic-statist tax reform. Like Wilson and McAdoo in 1916–17, Roosevelt and Secretary of the Treasury Morgenthau set out to finance a large fraction of the costs of war with taxation and to use taxes that bore heavily on corporations and upper-income groups.

The president began to prepare for financing mobilization as early as 1939, and he focused more on the issue of tax structure than on the level of taxation. He talked widely about the need for excess-profits taxation; in the summer of 1940 he proposed such a tax, to be steeply graduated, on both individuals and corporations. Roosevelt, the Treasury, the Ways and Means Committee, and Senate liberals such as Robert M. La Follette, Jr., favored a World War I–style tax on profits above a minimum rate of return. Pat Harrison and other conservative Democrats, however, opposed this and had the power to prevail. In the Second Revenue Act of 1940, passed in October, they established a graduated tax on excess profits, reaching a maximum of 50 percent, but provided a generous credit based on prewar profits. Secretary of the Interior Ickes complained that this was "abandoning advanced New Deal ground with a vengeance," but Roosevelt decided not to challenge the power of Congress by accusing it of having sold out to big business.[1]

In 1941, following the passage of the Lend-Lease Act, the Roosevelt administration faced growing inflationary pressures. In response to those pressures, as well as to the need for new revenues, Roosevelt and Morgenthau now supported lowering the exemptions from personal income and thus restraining consumption. But they did not abandon reform. Morgenthau proposed taxing away all corporate profits above a 6 percent rate of return, as well as increasing surtaxes on personal income, increasing the base for gift and estate taxes, and increasing excise taxes on beer, tobacco, and gasoline. Roosevelt made it clear he favored a massive elimination of personal income-tax deductions by switching to the taxation of gross income. But in the Revenue Act of 1941 Congress once again rejected most of the reform measures. The act's major provisions consisted of lower exemptions and higher tax rates on upper-middle-class families.

After Pearl Harbor, Morgenthau and Roosevelt resumed their bid for public support of tax reform. "In this time of grave national danger, when all excess income should go to win the war," Roosevelt told a joint session of Congress in 1942, "no American citizen ought to have a net income, after he has paid his taxes, of more than $25,000." But opposition to radical war-tax proposals grew even stronger in the face of the revenue requirements of full mobilization.

One source of opposition came from a diverse group of military planners, foreign-policy strategists, financial leaders, and economists. Throughout the turbulence of the 1920s and 1930s, these

---

[1] In June, Roosevelt had favored a graduated tax on all profits in excess of 4 percent. June 9, 1940, and August 10, 1940, entries in Harold Ickes Diaries, Ickes Papers.

experts had marshaled the economic lessons of World War I and its aftermath. Now, this collection of experts wanted to mobilize even greater resources, to do so more smoothly and predictably, and to reduce inflationary pressures. They promoted a policy of mass-based taxation. They favored a general sales tax or an income tax that produced most of its revenue from wages and salaries—one that would build on the successful performance of Social Security taxation. One of the leading experts was Russell C. Leffingwell, who had been assistant secretary of the Treasury during World War I and a partner in J. P. Morgan and Company since the early 1920s. He urged Morgenthau to avoid steep excess-profits taxation and to adopt, instead, "taxes widely spread on all the people." An income tax that not only was broad-based but also taxed people "to the very limit of endurance" was the core of successful war finance, he wrote to Morgenthau.[2]

The second source of opposition to Roosevelt's and Morgenthau's radical wartime tax proposals came, in sharp contrast with Wilson's situation during World War I, from Democrats in both Congress and the administration itself. Many Democratic members of Congress, especially the leadership of the Senate Finance Committee, shared the verdict of *Time* magazine, which warned that the kind of plan that Morgenthau proposed would put corporations in a "weakened financial position to meet the slump and unemployment that [would] come with peace." This same fear of postwar depression led Federal Reserve Chairman Marriner Eccles, Budget Director Harold Smith, Office of Price Administration Director Leon Henderson, and Vice President Henry Wallace to support the sales-taxation approach to war finance. Morgenthau complained that his opponents had forgotten about the "people in

---

[2] Leffingwell to Morgenthau, October 2, 1941, and June 11, 1942, Russell C. Leffingwell Papers, Yale University Library. This was part of an extensive wartime correspondence between Leffingwell and Morgenthau.

the lower one-third." He noted, "I can get all my New Dealers in the bathtub now."[3]

In the summer of 1942 Morgenthau, on the recommendation of Randolph Paul and Roy Blough, tried to bridge the gap between the administration and Congress by proposing the adoption of a sharply graduated spendings tax designed to raise large revenues and restrain consumption while increasing progressiveness. Adoption of such a tax would have been by far the most radical departure in American tax policy since 1916. The tax-writing committees regarded this proposal as too radical economically and too threatening to the influence they enjoyed as gatekeepers for the complex exemptions and deductions in the income tax. Roosevelt recognized the power of the committees, and regarded the spendings tax as a bargaining tool for defeating a general sales tax and for making the income tax more progressive. The president decided not to support Morgenthau, explaining to him that "I always have to have a couple of whipping boys."[4]

In October, Congress finally agreed to a few progressive concessions and settled on the income tax as the centerpiece of war finance. To be sure, the tax-writing committees demonstrated their power by refusing to adopt the World War I method of taxing corporate excess profits, although they did increase the rate of such taxation to 90 percent as a temporary wartime measure. The committees also protected major loopholes favoring the wealthy and provided less than half the revenues that Roosevelt had requested. But the Revenue Act of 1942 represented agreement between Congress and Roosevelt on what became the core of a new tax regime—a personal income tax that was both broadly based and progressive. The act made major reductions in personal exemptions, establishing the means for the federal government to

---

[3] Blum, *Morgenthau Diaries: Years of War*, 35.
[4] Blum, *Morgenthau Diaries: Years of War*, 48.

acquire huge revenues from the taxation of middle-class wages and salaries. Just as important, the rates on individuals' incomes— rates that included a surtax graduated from 13 percent on the first $2,000 to 82 percent on taxable income over $200,000—made the personal income tax more progressive than at any other time in its history. Once again, Roosevelt had defeated a general sales tax, just as he had in 1933, the last time significant support for one had surfaced. A highly progressive income tax, coupled with the absence of general sales taxation, was the major payoff from Roosevelt's earlier tax-reform campaigns, which had established widespread public expectations that any significant new taxes would be progressive. At the same time, Roosevelt and many New Deal legislators hoped to be able to distribute much of the new revenues in progressive fashion. They believed that a mass-based income tax would be the best way to ensure a permanent flow of revenues to federal programs of social justice.

Roosevelt continued his reform fight to make the income tax even more progressive, to tax corporations more heavily, and to shift revenue raising from borrowing to taxation, but he suffered two major defeats in 1943.

The first was over withholding.

In 1943, to accelerate the flow of tax revenues into the Treasury and thus restrain inflation, the Treasury proposed adopting a system for withholding taxes through monthly payroll deductions or quarterly payments. The federal government had already employed such a system of "collection at the source" during the Civil War (and again between 1913 and 1916) in an effort to replicate the administrative accomplishments of the British income tax. As early as 1911, the state of Wisconsin had employed a comprehensive system of acquiring "information at the source" from corporations to assess individual income taxes owed by salaried managers and skilled workers. More recently, the federal government had achieved great success with a "collection at the source" administrative system for Social Security taxes. Edwin E. Witte, who served as executive director for Roosevelt's Committee on Economic Security, which drafted the Social Security Act of 1935, had become intimately familiar with the Wisconsin system during his years as chief of Wisconsin's Legislative Reference Library. He may well have drawn from that experience in championing payroll taxation. By mid-1940 the Bureau of Old-Age Benefits had processed, without the benefit of electronic computers, more than 312 million individual wage reports forwarded by the Bureau of Internal Revenue and had posted over 99 percent of them to more than 50 million individual employee accounts.[5]

The proposed collection system would keep taxpayers current rather than allow them to pay the year after the taxes were incurred. Also, it would expedite taxpaying by citizens, such as most industrial workers, who had no experience in filing income-tax returns. Further, withholding promised to make it possible, for the first time, to vary income-tax rates and collections in an effective countercyclical fashion. The Keynesians within the Treasury had supported withholding at the source for that reason. Adoption of the plan meant, however, that during 1943 taxpayers would pay both their 1942 and their 1943 obligations.

One of the first to oppose the double payment was Beardsley Ruml, chairman of the New York Federal Reserve Bank and treasurer of R. H. Macy and Company. He launched a radio and press campaign to challenge the Treasury. He favored withholding but proposed the forgiveness of 1942 taxes to ease the pinch in 1943. Ruml's plan gained public support, but Roosevelt defended the

---

[5] Arthur J. Altmeyer, *The Formative Years of Social Security* (Madison: University of Wisconsin Press, 1963), 86–7. In 1916, the Wilson administration abandoned "collection at the source" in favor of Wisconsin's "information at the source." The Wilson administration was responding to pressure from large corporations, which received no compensation for their administrative costs, and was concerned that corporations were undercollecting individual income taxes. See Brownlee, "Wilson and Financing the Modern State," 196–7.

Treasury, telling the chair of the Ways and Means Committee, "I cannot acquiesce in the elimination of a whole year's tax burden on the upper income groups during a war period when I must call for an increase in taxes . . . from the mass of people." After some modest concessions to Roosevelt, Congress adopted the Ruml plan in the Current Tax Payment Act of 1943.

The second defeat for Roosevelt's wartime tax program occurred in the Revenue Act of 1943.

Led by the tax-writing committees, Congress rejected the Treasury's advice and passed legislation providing for only modest tax increases ($2.3 billion versus the $10.5 billion requested by the Treasury) while creating a host of new tax favors for business, especially the mining, timber, and steel industries. Roosevelt denounced the bill as "not a tax bill but a tax relief bill, providing relief not for the needy but for the greedy." He vetoed the bill, but for the first time in history, Congress overrode a presidential veto of a revenue act. Alben Barkley, the Democratic majority leader in the Senate, described Roosevelt's veto message as a "calculated and deliberate assault upon the legislative integrity of every member of Congress." Ickes hoped that Roosevelt would go "to the people with his case against the Congress" for enacting "a vicious bill designed to protect the rich at the expense of the poor."[6] But the humiliating defeat convinced Roosevelt that he had to accept the structure of the income taxation without further complaint. His defeats in 1943 essentially ended the conflict, which had begun during World War I between business and progressive advocates, over soak-the-rich income taxation.

Under the new tax system, the number of individual taxpayers grew from 3.9 million in 1939 to 42.6 million in 1945, and federal income-tax collections over the period leaped from $2.2 billion to $35.1 billion. By the end of the war nearly 90 percent of the

[6] February 26, 1944, entry, Harold Ickes Diaries, Ickes Papers.

members of the labor force submitted income-tax returns, and about 60 percent of the labor force paid income taxes. In 1944 and 1945, individual income taxes accounted for roughly 40 percent of federal revenues, whereas corporate income taxes provided about one-third—only half their share during World War I. Mass taxation had become more important than class taxation. At the same time, the federal government came to dominate the nation's revenue system. In 1940, federal income tax had accounted for only 16 percent of the taxes collected by all levels of government; by 1950 the federal income tax produced more than 51 percent of all collections. Installation of the new regime was the most dramatic shift in the nation's tax policies since 1916.

In making the new individual income tax work, the Roosevelt administration relied heavily on voluntarism by encouraging the self-reporting of income.[7] Roosevelt, Morgenthau, and the congressional leadership all were reluctant to impose a highly coercive system of assessment and collection. To be sure, payroll withholding was coercive, but it was popular in that it spread out payments over twelve months, reducing the pain of taxpaying, and it did not reach self-employed and many salaried workers.

The federal government won middle-class political support for, and compliance with, the new income tax in part because of the structure of the tax. General deductions (e.g., for interest on home mortgages and for payments of state and local taxes) sweetened the new tax system for the middle class. Moreover, middle-class taxpayers preferred the mass-based income tax to a national sales tax, which many corporate leaders favored and promoted. Fur-

---

[7] Scholars often call reliance on self-reporting an example of American exceptionalism in taxation. For international comparisons of income-tax administration, see Arnold J. Heidenheimer, Hugh Heclo, and Carolyn T. Adams, *Comparative Public Policy: The Politics of Social Choice in Europe and America* (New York: St. Martin's Press, 1975), 235–42.

thermore, fear of a renewed depression made the middle-class public more tolerant than it had been during World War I toward taxation that was favorable to corporations and corporate privilege. This leniency may have seemed naive to radical New Dealers, but it expressed a widely shared commitment to the pursuit of enlightened self-interest.

The new regime of mass taxation succeeded too because of the popularity of the war effort. It was less necessary to leverage popular support and sacrifice for the war by enacting a highly redistributional tax system. More so than in World War I, Americans concluded that their nation's security was at stake and that victory required both personal sacrifice through taxation and indulgence of the corporate profits that helped fuel the war machine.

But the Roosevelt administration believed that the new withholding system and the fundamental popularity of the new income tax were not enough to make mass-based taxation effective. The Roosevelt administration concluded that it had to go beyond shaping the tax code in ways that compelled or encouraged compliance. The administration had to persuade the public that the tax was fair, convenient, and for a necessary purpose. Roosevelt and Morgenthau invoked the extensive propaganda machinery at their command in a campaign to convince the millions of new taxpayers to pay tax obligations. The Treasury, its Bureau of Internal Revenue, and the Office of War Information launched a massive propaganda effort. In it, these agencies invoked the same calls for civic responsibility and patriotic sacrifice that the Wilson administration had crafted so effectively during the bond campaigns of World War I.

The Roosevelt administration made full use of the instruments of mass communication in promoting conscientious taxpaying. The Treasury commissioned Irving Berlin to write a song for the effort entitled "I Paid My Income Tax Today." The Treasury sent recordings of the song to radio stations and asked Danny Kaye to perform it in New York night clubs. The Treasury also commissioned a Disney animated short, "The New Spirit," starring Donald Duck. Informed by the radio that it is "your privilege, not just your duty . . . to help your government by paying your tax and paying it promptly," Donald gathers the supplies (including a bottle of aspirin) necessary to fill in his return. He finds the job easier and, with the exemptions and credits for his three nephews, less painful than he anticipated. The message was that the average citizen would find the new income taxes easy to pay. The film ends with Donald traveling to Washington to pay his tax in person, and to see how tax revenues are transformed into the arsenal of democracy. In early 1942, more than 32 million people in 12,000 theaters watched "The New Spirit."[8]

In the campaigns on behalf of mass-based income taxation, the Roosevelt administration demonstrated the power of presidential leadership. The Roosevelt administration persuaded at the same time as it coerced. Thus, during World War II, as well as in World War I and even in the Civil War, a liberal-democratic state demonstrated the fiscal power of a trusting and wealthy public.

---

[8] On the income-tax advertising campaigns, see Carolyn C. Jones, "Class Tax to Mass Tax: The Rise of Propaganda in the Expansion of the Income Tax during World War II," *Buffalo Law Review* 37 (1989): 685–737; Jones, "Taxes to Beat the Axis: A Comparison of American and British Income Tax Publicity during World War II," paper prepared for presentation at the Tenth International Economic History Congress, Leuven, Belgium, June 12, 1990; and Jones, "Mass-Based Income Taxation: Creating a Taxpaying Culture, 1940–1952," in Brownlee, ed., *Funding the Modern American State,* 108–48. These campaigns ought to be set in the context of all of the propaganda efforts by the Roosevelt administration. Mark Leff has usefully suggested viewing such campaigns as part of the "politics of sacrifice." But as in his study of New Deal tax policy, Leff neglects the substantial, as opposed to a purely symbolic, interest of Roosevelt and Morgenthau in increasing the sacrifice of corporations and the wealthy. Mark Leff, "The Politics of Sacrifice on the Home Front in World War II," *Journal of American History* 77 (March 1991): 1296–318.

That trust, nurtured by the federal government, permitted and encouraged the adoption of income taxation, which is, along with property taxation, the most coercive and statist means of raising revenue. Perhaps only the liberal-democratic states can impose coercive taxation in a sustained fashion—and still survive in the long run. In any event, American government overcame any structural weaknesses during World War II, just as during the two earlier emergencies of the Civil War and World War I. In a fiscal sense, the adoption of mass-based income taxation during World War II—and the victory of a taxpaying culture—represented a triumph for both the republican virtue and the national strength the framers of the Constitution had sought to advance.

Because of the buoyant revenues produced under the new tax regime, during the last two years of World War II the federal government covered roughly half of its expenditures with tax revenues. In addition, the federal deficit, after increasing from $6.2 billion in 1941 to $57.4 billion in 1943, held at about the 1943 level for the remainder of the war. These were impressive feats because the wartime expenditures represented a more massive shift of resources from peacetime endeavors than had been the case during World War I. The average level of wartime federal expenditures, which increased from 1942 through 1945, amounted to roughly half the national product—more than twice the average ratio during World War I. In addition, the shift of resources was faster and more prolonged. At the same time, the fact that the federal government had hitched taxation more firmly to expenditure needs and dramatically broadened the tax base helped restrain wartime price inflation.

SURVIVAL OF THE REGIME AFTER THE WAR

The winning of World War II and a postwar surge of economic prosperity, which followed so closely on the heels of the Great

Depression, all helped produce a popular, bipartisan consensus of support for sustaining the basic policy shifts undertaken during the Roosevelt administration. One expression of this consensus was the congressional passage of the Employment Act of 1946. This was a formal commitment by the federal government to what was believed to have been the implicit fiscal policy of Franklin Roosevelt. The act, in fact, captured three important elements in Roosevelt's fiscal policy. First, it declared the federal government's central responsibility for managing the level of employment. Second, by creating the Council of Economic Advisers and charging it with the development of an annual published report (*The Economic Report of the President*), the act established that the president and the public should have economic advice that was expert and independent. And third, it formally embodied a central objective of the New Deal: to embrace human values as the context for setting and evaluating fiscal policy. The institutional framework was in place for the proactive manipulation of the federal budget on behalf of economic stability.

Like Roosevelt's real fiscal policy, however, the act provided policymakers with little guidance on the substance of fiscal policy. It failed to make a government guarantee of full employment; it restricted countercyclical actions to only those consistent with other economic objectives; and it avoided a specific definition of appropriate policy. Keynesian ideas had won a larger audience during World War II, but public-finance experts sharply disagreed over the content of countercyclical policy. Some regarded the conjunction of great deficits and dramatic economic expansion as proof that deficits not only had produced the economic expansion of World War II, ending the Great Depression, but also were required for sustained prosperity in peacetime. Other experts, such as the leadership of the Committee for Economic Development (CED), which represented businesspeople interested in Keynesianism, had a more conservative view. In 1947 the CED issued a statement on fiscal policy, *Taxes and the Budget,* which accepted deficits during recessions but advocated budget surpluses during times of high employment and stable rates of taxation.[9]

In the realm of tax policy, the World War II emergency institutionalized a new tax regime. It had three elements: (1) a progressive but mass-based personal income tax for general revenues; (2) a flat-rate tax on corporate income, also for general revenues; and (3) a regressive payroll tax for social insurance. Although some important differences remained between the two major political parties, both insisted on maintaining the central characteristics of the World War II revenue system and eschewing both progressive assaults on corporate financial structures and the regressive taxation of consumption. For the first time since the early nineteenth century, the two political parties agreed on the essential elements of the nation's fiscal policy.

The general decline of partisanship after World War II no doubt contributed to the convergence of the two parties on fiscal policy. The convergence on tax policy involved acceptance by the Republican Party of higher levels of taxation of corporate profits and large incomes, levels that the business community had regarded as unconscionable at the time World War II ended. (The postwar tax on corporate incomes reached a peak of 52 percent, which held until 1964; thereafter, until 1986, it was usually either 46 percent or 48 percent.) But the convergence was more the product of a shift in direction by the Democratic Party. In the postwar era, Democrats largely abandoned taxation as an instrument to mobilize class interests. Although Presidents John F. Kennedy and Lyndon B. Johnson continued to support tax reforms, such as the taxation of capital gains at death, they also advocated a variety of tax cuts and did so by hawking the "supply-side" benefits in ways

---

[9] On the 1947 report of the CED, see Stein, *Fiscal Revolution in America,* 220–40.

reminiscent of Andrew Mellon. In 1964, Congress responded to Johnson's call for a tax cut "to increase our national income and Federal revenues" by slashing taxes in the face of large deficits. The Council of Economic Advisers, also committed to "growthmanship," actively supported the 1964 cuts, which reduced capital-gains taxes and allowed more generous depreciation allowances. Most liberals regarded the 1964 tax cuts as a victory for aggressive countercyclical stimulation of demand; they also embraced a conservative supply-side rationale for the cuts.

Thus, Democrats assisted the Republican Party in finishing the job it had begun during the 1920s: taking both the partisan sting and the redistributional threat out of taxation. The shift in the tax policy favored by the Democratic Party was part of its more general shift—one begun after 1937, accelerated during World War II, and completed in the Kennedy-Johnson era—away from democratic statism and toward corporate liberalism. This line of thinking had expanded its intellectual ambit, and its political potency, by incorporating Keynesian countercyclical policies. Presidents Kennedy and Johnson invoked Keynesian ideas as part of a strategy for winning business support for their tax-reform program.[10]

The bipartisan consensus ushered in an era of buoyant public finance that lasted until the 1980s. Usually well removed from the

---

[10] The scholarly literature on the Kennedy-Johnson tax programs has become impressive in depth and scope. See, for example, King, *Money, Time and Politics,* 151–319; Cathie Jo Martin, *Shifting the Burden: The Struggle Over Growth and Corporate Taxation* (Chicago: University of Chicago Press, 1991); Martin, "American Business and the Taxing State: Alliances for Growth in the Postwar Period," in Brownlee, ed., *Funding the Modern American State,* 354–407; Stein, *Fiscal Revolution in America,* 372–453; Witte, *Politics and Development of the Federal Income Tax,* 155–75; and Julian Zelizer, "Learning the Ways and Means: Wilbur Mills and a Fiscal Community, 1954–1964," in Brownlee, ed., *Funding the Modern American State,* 290–353.

contested turf of partisan politics, the tax policies and political actions that produced the era were nearly invisible.

Democrats and Republicans generally reached a consensus over the need for support of effective income-tax administration, and kept issues surrounding tax administration out of politics. During the presidency of Harry Truman, both Democratic and Republican leaders saw withholding as crucial to the success of the income tax. They supported ensuring adequate funding for the BIR, including its efforts to punish employers who refused to withhold taxes.

The Truman administration shifted enforcement emphasis from the tax dodges of established fortunes to the "tax chiseling" of those who had profited during wartime and the period of prosperity following the war. In a 1947 *Collier's* article, Undersecretary of the Treasury A. L. M. Wiggins described how the BIR had sent 128 revenue agents to a farming community in Minnesota to examine bank accounts, store accounts, government payments, crop yields, and the records of grain and cattle buyers. Wiggins reported that the BIR had collected over $5 million in additional taxes and penalties from farmers in that community. The Treasury and the BIR did not reveal that, although they were increasing the efforts to audit individuals, efforts such as the Minnesota investigation were unusual. They wanted those tax dodgers who were, in Commissioner of Internal Revenue George Schoeneman's words, "a tragic group of otherwise respectable individuals" to fear apprehension and punishment.

To that end, Wiggins and Schoeneman exaggerated the efficiency of the BIR. In 1949, Schoeneman told the readers of *American Magazine* that "You see, it's almost impossible to deceive our investigators, because most of them are generally familiar with every type of dodge ever attempted, and if they run across what appears to be a new one, they can look into the files and find it's been tried before." The Treasury had used propaganda to stress patriotic values during World War II. In the postwar era, it used the mass media to deliver threats. Fear of the Bureau of Internal Revenue (renamed the Internal Revenue Service in 1953), combined with the political popularity of the individual income tax, led to what was, by worldwide standards, an unusually high level of taxpayer compliance.[11]

An equally central but more veiled element of the era of easy finance was an expansive system of Social Security. With remarkably little public debate, and with bipartisan agreement, the federal government embraced a policy of steadily raising Social Security tax rates. Roosevelt's institutional legacy was part of the reason for the success of Social Security proponents in raising taxes during peacetime. His strategy of earmarking tax revenues for Social Security helped defeat pluralist hostility to increasing taxes.

Crucial as well to the expansion of Social Security was a policy network that formed around the Social Security experts who were in government. A professionally diverse set of experts in the Social Security Administration, including Arthur Altmeyer, Robert Ball, and Wilbur J. Cohen, not only provided substantial intellectual contributions to the analytical understanding of Social Security but also acted as policy entrepreneurs. These experts created a network of allies elsewhere in the government and beyond, within the public at large. This "Social Security crowd" began defending

---

[11] A. L. M. Wiggins, "They Can't Fool the Internal Revenue Man," *Collier's*, September 1947; George Schoeneman, "Tax Cheaters Beware!" *American Magazine*, February 1949. On the postwar enforcement efforts, see Jones, "Mass-Based Income Taxation," in Brownlee, ed., *Funding the Modern American State.* We do not have a scholarly history of the Internal Revenue Service and the BIR, but for a very useful reference work, see Shelley L. Davis, *IRS Historical Fact Book: A Chronology, 1646–1992* (Washington, D.C.: U.S. Government Printing Office, 1992).

the system against political threats during the 1930s and 1940s. Some of the threats came at the hands of Keynesian economists who criticized the system's accumulation of funds as deflationary. The Social Security network advanced programs incrementally but in 1950 it also engineered a major expansion of program coverage (including, for the first time, self-employed persons) and payroll taxation. In the next decade the network won strong bipartisan and congressional support, including that of House Ways and Means chair Wilbur Mills, for their accomplishments, and for further expansion of the system.

Increases in the tax base, as well as higher tax rates, boosted Social Security revenues. Steady and often dramatic economic growth—defined as growth in productivity—meant that payroll taxation tended to produce greater per-capita levels of tax revenues. Social Security taxes increased from iess than 1 percent of GNP in the late 1940s to more than 7 percent by the late 1970s. With this funding, Social Security payments increased from $472 million in 1946 (less than 1 percent of GNP) to $105 billion in 1979 (about 4.3 percent of GNP).[12]

Persistent inflation, as well as economic growth, helped to extend the life of the World War II tax regime. This inflation was another silent source of growing fiscal capacity. Inflation peaked first in the late 1940s, then increased again during the late 1960s and continued throughout the 1970s. This inflation reduced the value of outstanding debt and thereby played a role of unprecedented proportions in financing the federal government. Inflation also produced "bracket creep," or the push of increasing numbers of families into higher tax brackets faster than their real incomes increased. Thus the structure of income-tax rates became substan-

---

[12] On the postwar expansion of the Social Security system, see Edward D. Berkowitz, "Social Security and the Financing of the American State," in Brownlee, ed., *Funding the Modern American State,* 149–94.

tially more progressive, especially at the higher levels of income. The same effect, coupled with a failure to increase the personal exemption as rapidly as prices rose, propelled many low-income families into the tax system. By the early 1980s the portion of the labor force paying taxes had increased to more than 75 percent from the 60 percent level reached at the end of World War II. Meanwhile, the corporate income tax, with a flat rate and hence no bracket creep, became a less dynamic source of revenue. In 1950, individual and corporate income-tax revenues were roughly equal; by 1980, individual income-tax revenues were nearly four times as large as corporate.[13]

Because of unanticipated inflation, the revenue system proved to be far more elastic after World War II than experts had predicted. Economists at the CED, for example, had believed that after the war, federal tax receipts as a share of gross domestic product would fall from the wartime peak of 22 percent to somewhere between 10 and 15 percent. In fact, the tax share of national product dipped below 15 percent only briefly, in 1950. By 1952 it was approaching 20 percent and ever since has remained close to, or slightly above, 20 percent.[14]

The combination of growth in productivity and inflation meant that the federal government often could respond positively to requests for new programs without enacting politically damaging tax increases. The highly elastic revenue system paid for the strategic defense programs of the Cold War and, without any general or permanent increases in income taxation, for the mobilizations for the Korean and Vietnam Wars as well. But the size of the defense

---

[13] For a summary of the operation of postwar individual income tax, including the trends in progressiveness, see Jon Bakija and Eugene Steuerle, "Individual Income Taxation since 1948," *National Tax Journal* 44 (December 1991): 451–75.

[14] Herbert Stein provided the information regarding the CED estimates at the end of World War II. Stein to Brownlee, June 20, 1994.

budget relative to GNP tended to decline through the 1970s, except during the Korean and Vietnam Wars. Thus, the post–World War II increases in federal revenues went largely for the expansion of domestic programs—education, welfare, health services (including Medicare), urban redevelopment, and the channeling of federal revenues to state and local governments through indirect methods such as grants-in-aid and revenue sharing.

The federal government expanded intergovernmental support based on the programs developed after the Civil War, after World War I, and during the New Deal. Federal grants declined in importance during the 1940s, increased modestly during the 1950s, and then grew swiftly during the 1960s and 1970s. In these two decades, revenue sharing—federal subsidies to state and local governments without programmatic strings—dominated. By 1974, more than 20 percent of state and local revenues came from federal aid, which amounted to a kind of tax relief to state and local governments. Following World War II, state and local tax receipts had increased even more rapidly than had federal taxes. State and local taxes almost doubled as a percentage of GNP, rising to almost 10 percent of GNP by 1972.

The inflation-driven increases in revenues also permitted new "tax expenditures"—special preferences offered under the tax code in the form of exclusions, deductions, and credits. Tax expenditures that benefited middle-class taxpayers had accompanied the introduction and expansion of mass-based income taxation during the 1940s and 1950s. After World War II, and the ebbing of patriotism as a factor in income-tax compliance, Congress relied increasingly on tax expenditures and other measures—including the introduction of the income-splitting joint return for husbands and wives and the acceptance of community-property status—to enhance the legitimacy of the new tax regime. However, a deduction that had been in the tax code since 1913—the deduction for mortgage interest—was the most expensive of the tax expenditures.[15]

During the 1960s and 1970s, tax expenditures became even more popular, and both old and new forms grew relative to conventional expenditures. Politicians became attracted to tax expenditures as a way to accomplish social goals—such as the promotion of home ownership embedded in the deduction of mortgage interest—without having to make large and politically difficult direct expenditures of funds. In other words, many Democratic and Republican members of Congress found self-serving political benefits in hiding tax programs from public scrutiny. Contributing to the movement as well were taxpaying groups that aggressively sought preferential treatment within the tax code in order to offset the effects of bracket creep. In turn, the taxpayers and legislators who benefited from the tax expenditures developed a vested interest in increasing the complexity of the process of tax legislation.[16]

Although the general public was slow to recognize the significance of tax expenditures, a group of tax lawyers and economists struggled to expose the inequities resulting from increasing exemptions and deductions. Especially influential were the economist Joseph Pechman and the law professor Stanley Surrey. They drew on a line of analysis that had its roots in the arguments of the economists Thomas S. Adams, Robert Murray Haig, and Henry Simons, who during the 1920s and 1930s had suggested that the federal government ought to rationalize the personal income tax by basing it on a comprehensive, economic definition of income—

---

[15] On the joint return and community-property status, see Jones, "Mass-Based Income Taxation," in Brownlee, ed., *Funding the Modern American State.*

[16] The leading analysis of the bureaucratic complexity of making tax policy, especially within Congress, during the 1960s and 1970s is Reese, *Politics of Taxation.*

one that measured, in Haig's words, "the money value of the net accretion of one's economic power between two points in time." Adopting Haig's definition for the purposes of income taxation would require the taxing of items such as net capital gains and the income-in-kind that an owner enjoys from an owner-occupied residence.[17]

Base-broadening won a wider audience during World War II when the CED commissioned Henry Simons to develop a reform program focused on expanding the definition of taxable income. In 1959, Congressman Wilbur Mills, chair of the House Ways and Means Committee, held hearings and published papers that put base-broadening reforms on the agenda of a new fiscal community that coalesced in the late 1950s and early 1960s. By acting as a broker between fiscal experts and the larger political world, Mills promoted coherent policymaking within the complex administrative state created by the New Deal and World War II. As a consequence of the influence of Mills and other experts, the Revenue Act of 1962 contained a few base-broadening reforms, such as restrictions on foreign tax havens, on benefits for cooperatives, and on travel and entertainment deductions.[18]

---

[17] Robert M. Haig, "The Concept of Income," in Haig, ed., *The Federal Income Tax* (New York: Columbia University Press, 1921), 7.

[18] For a summary of the base-broadening movement, see Joseph A. Pechman, "Tax Reform: Theory and Practice," *Journal of Economic Perspectives* I (Summer 1987): 11–28. The CED published Simons's program in 1944 as Committee for Economic Development, *A Post-war Federal Tax Plan for High Employment* (New York: CED, 1944). Simons later published an elaborate version of his plan. See Henry C. Simons, *Federal Tax Reform* (Chicago: University of Chicago Press, 1950). For an assessment of Simons's contributions to tax theory, see Harold Groves, *Tax Philosophers: Two Hundred Years of Thought in Great Britain and the United States*, edited by Donald J. Curran (Madison: University of Wisconsin Press, 1974), 74–85. For the influential hearings sponsored by Wilbur Mills, see U.S. House of Representatives, Committee on Ways and Means, *Tax*

Beginning in 1967, Surrey, as assistant secretary of the treasury (1961–69), further enhanced the visibility of base broadening by introducing the organizing concept of tax expenditures.[19] He led in articulating the Treasury's position that the government should pursue social goals openly, through direct expenditures. Surrey, economists within the Treasury, and a string of Treasury assistant secretaries and commissioners of internal revenue who favored base-broadening worked in ways that would have pleased Thomas S. Adams. From within the Treasury they highlighted the massive size of tax expenditures and underscored the kind of economic inefficiencies, distortions, and unfairness that the tax expenditures created. In 1974, the Congressional Budget Act acknowledged the importance of the concept and advanced the debate by requiring the annual publication of a "tax-expenditure budget." Subsequently the Congressional Budget Office estimated that in 1967, tax expenditures cost the federal government nearly $37 billion (equal to 21 percent of federal expenditures) and that the total cost had soared to $327 billion by 1984 (equal to 35 percent of federal expenditures).[20]

Revision Compendium: Compendium of Papers on Broadening the Tax Base, two volumes (Washington, D.C.: U.S. Government Printing Office, 1959). On Mills's interest in base-broadening reform, see Zelizer, "Learning the Ways and Means," in Brownlee, ed., *Funding the Modern American State.* It should be noted that Pechman lent support to Zelizer's interpretation of Mills by crediting Mills with boosting the cause of comprehensive personal-income taxation. See Pechman, "Tax Reform: Theory and Practice," 12.

[19] For a discussion of Surrey's views, including his 1967 proposal of a "tax-expenditure budget," see Stanley S. Surrey, *Pathways to Tax Reform: The Concept of Tax Expenditures* (Cambridge, Mass.: Harvard University Press, 1973).

[20] Such expenditures ought to be incorporated in any systematic analysis of the long-term relationship between tax and expenditure policies. Just as tax expenditures mask the social effects of tax policy from the polity at large, they may make it difficult for social scientists to identify the "sand-

In the presidential campaign of 1976, Democratic candidate Jimmy Carter responded to the growing awareness of the incoherence of federal income taxation by calling the American tax system "a disgrace." He promised to make the federal income tax more progressive, to broaden its base, and to avoid "a piecemeal approach to change." But during his first two years in office, Carter found himself embroiled in piecemeal change and frustrated in his efforts to reduce the taxes of lower-income families. Congress insisted on avoiding tax cuts that might stimulate consumption and inflation. It concentrated instead on encouraging business investment to dampen inflation and foster productivity growth, which had slowed during the 1970s. Congress prevailed in the end, and President Carter reluctantly signed the Revenue Act of 1978. The act provided only minimal tax relief and simplification for individuals, but it offered generous cuts in capital gains and business taxes.

Congress failed to enact reform during the Carter administration, but it did entertain the creation of a new tax—a value-added tax on consumption—as part of a possible comprehensive overhaul of the federal tax system. For each transaction in the chain of production, the tax would apply a small levy to the value added in that step—the difference between the sale price of the product or service and the cost of the goods and services purchased to create the product or service. France had adopted

box" effects of tax policy. (In 1981 Secretary of the Treasury Donald Regan commented that "My favorite part of the tax bill is the indexing provision—it takes the sand out of Congress's sandbox.") The growing significance of "tax expenditures" during the 1970s may help account, institutionally, for the disappearance of the "causal" association between taxation and expenditures noted by Hoover and Sheffrin during that decade. See Kevin D. Hoover and Steven Sheffrin, "Causation, Spending, and Taxes: Sand in the Sandbox or Tax Collector for the Welfare State?" *American Economic Review* 82 (March 1992): 225–48.

a value-added tax as early as 1954, and between 1967 and 1973 all of the members of the European Economic Community, including Great Britain, adopted it as their standard form of sales taxation.

In 1978 Senator Russell Long, chair of the Senate Finance Committee, proposed substituting value-added taxation for income and Social Security taxes. Then Al Ullman, a Democratic representative from Oregon and chair of the House Ways and Means Committee, introduced a concrete plan to move in that direction. For the first time since 1940, Congress looked closely at comprehensive taxation of consumption.

At the time, Ullman's proposed Tax Reconstruction Act of 1980 was probably the most radical approach to tax reform seriously considered by Congress since World War II. However, liberals worried about its regressiveness, and conservatives, including business leaders, argued that the new tax would encourage the growth of government. Together, they prevented the bill from coming to a vote. Meanwhile, Oregon voters, who apparently disliked the prospect of new taxes, especially on consumption, ended Ullman's congressional career. Once again, just as at earlier junctures, the federal government stopped short of encouraging savings and investment through the comprehensive taxation of consumption. Only the high-tariff system of the late nineteenth century stands as a possible exception to this pattern. But the central motivation for the tariff system had little to do with the stimulation of savings; it was designed primarily to manipulate international prices of manufactured goods and labor.

Carter's emphasis on redistributing the tax burden and Ullman's campaign for a new tax put them both at odds with a growing antigovernment movement. The movement was founded on concerns about the rising costs of government, widespread doubts about the effectiveness of governmental solutions to social problems, dissatisfaction over the quality of public services, and distrust of legislatures. Hostility to taxation often gave the movement a policy focus.

The antigovernment movement focused at first not so much on federal taxation as on state and local taxation, which taxpayers often felt more directly, and which grassroots organizing could more easily attack. The movement gained its most dramatic expression in a 1978 taxpayers' revolt in California. In a referendum, California voters approved Proposition 13, amending the state's constitution to limit the property-tax rate to 1 percent of market value, and to require a two-thirds majority of each house of the legislature to enact any new taxes. Stimulated by the success of Proposition 13, coalitions similar to the one that had formed in California—a combination of homeowners and owners of commercial property trying to reduce their tax bills, conservatives attacking welfare, liberals seeking a more progressive tax system, and people simply striking out at modern life—formed in a number of other states. The measures they framed were not as drastic as Proposition 13, but all were in its spirit and most survived state-level referenda and court challenges.[21]

Opposition to government spending and taxing quickly reached the federal level. A tax-reform movement gathered momentum, winning support in diverse quarters. Conservatives focused on bracket creep while liberal tax experts exposed the inequities resulting from increasing exemptions and deductions. Meanwhile, the nationwide tax revolt contributed to the nomination and election of President Ronald Reagan in 1980.

---

[21] There is a substantial literature on the Proposition 13 movement. See, for example, Arthur O'Sullivan, Terri A. Sexton, and Steven M. Sheffrin, *Property Taxes and Tax Revolts: The Legacy of Proposition 13* (Cambridge: Cambridge University Press, 1995); Alvin Rabushka and Pauline Ryan, *The Tax Revolt* (Stanford: Hoover Institution, 1982); and David O. Sears and Jack Citrin, *Tax Revolt: Something for Nothing in California* (Cambridge, Mass.: Harvard University Press, 1982).

THE REAGAN "REVOLUTION"

The era of buoyant revenues for domestic programs came to a quick end during the 1980s. The major source of its demise was a shift in tax policy: the sharp reduction of taxes associated with the Reagan "revolution."

Even without the historically contingent tax cuts of the first Reagan administration, however, changing economic circumstances would have undermined the era of easy finance. Until the late 1970s robust economic institutions and inflationary conditions had provided a powerful engine for tax revenues. From World War II to the late 1970s, both economic growth and long-term inflation created the fundamental conditions that enabled the federal government to garner increasing revenues and, as a consequence, to reduce corporate taxes and excise taxes and to avoid the politically damaging process of increasing tax rates. But during the late 1970s, the Federal Reserve began to attack inflation. The resulting decline of inflation in the 1980s, along with the weakening productivity that had ensued during the 1970s, undermined the "easy financing" period of the post-1941 fiscal regime. Economic trends pushed the makers of fiscal policy toward reliance on deficit financing and toward reduction of tax expenditures.

The role of the Reagan administration, however, was decisive. It undertook a massive reduction of taxes through the passage of the Economic Recovery Tax Act of 1981 (ERTA), which may well have been the most powerful part of the Reagan revolution. Its impact was international as well as domestic; along with Margaret Thatcher's tax reforms in Great Britain, it inspired a rate-lowering movement of income-tax reform that swept through Europe and Japan during the 1980s. The political basis for ERTA was Republican control of the Senate, conservative domination of the House, and growing popular enthusiasm for tax cutting.

President Reagan rationalized the tax cutting as supply-side stimulation of economic expansion, productivity, and even tax revenues. His personal views reinforced the popular enthusiasm for tax cutting, and did so in a particularly powerful way, because Reagan's supply-side ideas encountered no effective intellectual resistance.

Within the Reagan administration, conservative public-finance economists such as Harvard University's Martin Feldstein, who became chair of the Council of Economic Advisers later in the Reagan administration, and Stanford University's Michael Boskin, who served in the same position in the administration of George Bush, doubted supply-side economics. They did not believe that high taxation was central to the nation's economic ills or that drastic cutting would balance the budget, as economist Arthur Laffer argued. But they did want tax reform: reductions in tax rates that would improve economic incentives. Their desire for less progressive rates, coupled with their general support for the Reagan administration, meant that their reservations about supply-side economics had little effect outside the academic community.[22]

Those economists and politicians who doubted that supply-side economics would work and believed that large deficits would result from ERTA had little leverage to advance their concerns because the federal government had already abandoned a disciplined fiscal policy—a fiscal policy conforming to a rule or set of rules governing the size of the federal deficit. The consensus established in the early 1960s within the federal government behind a rule—the rule that tax and spending policies should pro-

---

[22] For the influence of both mainstream economists and "supply-siders" on the policies of the Reagan administration, see Paul Krugman, *Peddling Prosperity: Economic Sense and Nonsense in the Age of Diminished Expectations* (New York: W. W. Norton, 1994).

duce a balanced budget if the economy were operating at full employment—broke down later in that decade. In 1971, Richard Nixon formally abandoned the rule. He wanted to balance the full-employment budget but competing economic and political objectives forced him to abandon the goal. In 1974, when Herbert Stein convened President Gerald Ford's Council of Economic Advisers, he found that no one "had a credible theory of fiscal policy." By 1981, few in power believed, in Stein's words, "that there was some precise, knowable size of the deficit that was consistent with the stability of the economy."

ERTA's key provisions—indexing of income-tax rates for inflation and severe slashing of personal and business taxes—ensured the end of dynamic federal tax revenues. Herbert Stein has captured its significance by calling it the "Big Budget Bang." ERTA may not have initiated a new fiscal regime, but as Stein suggests, it has dominated fiscal policy ever since.[23]

ERTA reduced the role of the income tax in the nation's revenue system for the first time since the Great Depression. By 1990, indexing alone had reduced federal revenues by about $180 billion

[23] In an essay that continues his career-long interest in the evaluation of fiscal policy, Stein describes how the federal government, beginning as early as 1965, abandoned a coherent "aggregate rule" for setting countercyclical fiscal policy, including taxes. Stein has concluded that in 1969 he was premature, at best, when he declared, in *The Fiscal Revolution in America*, that "domesticated Keynesianism" had triumphed in 1962–4. In fact, Stein now finds that during the last thirty years, not one of the major approaches to budget balancing has prevailed. During the last thirty years, Stein argues, policymakers have been unwilling "to subordinate their desires for specific tax and expenditure programs to any aggregate goal." The simple obstacle to coherent fiscal policy, he suggests, is that "people—politicians and private citizens—cared about the ingredients of the budget for other reasons in addition to their cyclical consequences" and that "almost all were opposed to raising taxes most of the time." See Herbert Stein, "The Fiscal Revolution in America, Part II: 1964 to 1994," in Brownlee, ed., *Funding the Modern American State*, 195–287.

a year, and the ERTA rate reductions cost the Treasury an additional $80 billion annually. Meanwhile, income-tax revenues as a share of all federal taxes declined from 63 percent in 1980 to 57 percent in 1990. During the early 1980s, largely as a consequence of ERTA, relatively invisible, politically low-cost means of increasing tax revenues had vanished. For the moment, the Reagan revolution appeared to have succeeded in breaking the "upward ratchet" of federal taxation.[24]

The rapidly increasing budget deficits (roughly the size of the ERTA reductions in revenue) and interest payments began to restrain domestic spending. In response to the deficits, Congress took extraordinary action, passing the Gramm-Rudman-Hollings Act in 1985, which imposed automatic spending reductions (*but not tax increases*) whenever the deficit exceeded prescribed levels. Gramm-Rudman had some disciplinary effect, but deficits continued to increase into the 1990s.

Fiscal weakness also began to plague the Social Security system. Fiscal problems actually began during the 1970s, when benefits, which were indexed to prices, rose far more rapidly than wages and employment. By 1983 the old-age and survivors' trust fund had shrunk to half the size it had been in 1972. In 1983 a bipartisan group in Congress, working with Social Security loyalists,

---

[24] But at least one of the central participants from the Reagan administration in the passage of the 1981 legislation denies that the tax cut was a deliberate effort to create deficits. See David A. Stockman, *The Triumph of Politics: Why the Reagan Revolution Failed* (New York: Harper & Row, 1986), especially 229–68. Stockman's interpretation, reinforced by recent memoirs and well-researched journalism, is that the deficits were simply the result of the president's stubborn refusal to lend serious support to the cutting of expenditures. The memoirs are Donald T. Regan, *For the Record: From Wall Street to Washington* (New York: Harcout Brace Jovanovich, 1998), and Martin Anderson, *Revolution* (San Diego: Harcourt, 1988); the journalism is Lou Cannon, *President Reagan: The Role of a Lifetime* (New York: Simon & Schuster, 1991), 253–60.

experts in the Treasury, and the leadership of the Reagan administration, fashioned a compromise solution, which included a permanent reduction in Social Security benefits, an acceleration of previously scheduled increases in rates of Social Security taxation, and an expansion of the tax base. This compromise, coupled with the relatively small numbers of retirees in the 1990s (largely children of the Depression era), produced a strong rate of recovery of the trust fund.

During 1984 and 1985, while the crisis of the budget deficit mounted, Republicans and Democrats, both supported by Treasury staff, edged into a competitive scramble to occupy the high ground of tax reform. Republicans who sought to reduce tax rates on the wealthy initiated the movement that led to the 1986 measure, just as they had begun the movements that produced ERTA and the tax reforms of the 1920s. Particularly important in initiating the process that culminated in the 1986 reforms was a group of congressional Republicans, led by Jack Kemp, who favored continued tax cuts to stimulate productivity. But the rest of the process was very different from earlier Republican-sponsored reforms.[25]

One departure was that liberal Democrats now participated significantly. Senator Bill Bradley (D-New Jersey) played a particularly crucial, creative role in the drama. As early as 1982, Bradley, inspired in part by Stanley Surrey's earlier reform program, became enthusiastic about broadening the base of income taxation.

---

[25] The following account of the passage of the Tax Reform Act of 1986 draws on the excellent descriptions found in Jeffrey H. Birnbaum and Alan S. Murray, *Showdown at Gucci Gulch: Lawmakers, Lobbyists, and the Unlikely Triumph of Tax Reform* (New York: Random House, 1987); Timothy J. Conlan, Margaret T. Wrightson, and David R. Beam, *Taxing Choices: The Politics of Tax Reform* (Washington, D.C.: Congressional Quarterly Press, 1990); and C. Eugene Steuerle, *The Tax Decade* (Washington, D.C.: Urban Institute Press, 1992), 71–162.

He became convinced that the idea made economic sense, and that Democratic sponsorship of such reform would have voter appeal. In 1982, Bradley drew effectively on the advice of experts such as economists Joseph Minarik from the Congressional Budget Office and Randy Weiss, who was on the staff of the Joint Committee on taxation, to draft a base-broadening bill. But Bradley and his coauthor, Congressman Richard Gephardt, failed to win support from the party leadership, including presidential candidate Walter Mondale, who emphasized tax increases rather than tax reform in his 1984 campaign. Bradley was a member of the Senate Finance Committee, but until 1986 his hostility to tax expenditures made him an outsider within the committee.

The Republican administration also played a rather different role than Republican administrations had in the 1920s. The Reagan administration developed new goals, ones quite different from those emphasized by Republicans before. It became more interested in improving economic incentives for enterprise capitalism than in protecting corporate bureaucracies or the real-estate industry. Thus, the Reagan administration adopted a very different posture from the loophole-carving Republican administrations of the 1920s. Reagan himself was a factor in emphasizing enterprise capitalism and even increasing corporate taxes. His experience in the movie industry, like Bradley's in professional athletics, gave him a distaste for highly progressive rates on individual incomes, and his sense of fairness led him to doubt the equity of large tax expenditures that allowed certain corporations to go essentially tax-free.

Secretary of the Treasury Donald Regan was in general agreement on the issue of tax expenditures. In fact, he was probably more effective than anyone else in keeping the president on a reform track that included eliminating tax expenditures. Regan knew that the president had little personal knowledge of, or expe-

rience with, tax loopholes, so when he presented the president
with the first set of Treasury proposals (Treasury I) in November
1984, he asked Reagan how much tax he had paid before he
became president. Reagan reported a large figure. "Sucker," Regan
replied. He added:

With the right lawyer and the right accountant and the right tax
shelters, you needn't have paid a penny in taxes even if you made
more than a million dollars a year—and it would have been perfectly
legal and proper. The tax system we have now is designed to make
the avoidance of taxes easy for the rich and has the effect of making
it almost impossible for people who work for wages and salaries to
do the same.[26]

Regan's concern was not solely for equitable treatment of the
middle-class taxpayer. His years on Wall Street as a broker led
him to favor tax reform that would remove tax shelters that
drew investment capital away from more productive activities. He
recalled that he had "chafed under laws that gave the banking
industry tax breaks that brokerage firms were denied," and
stressed that "when the same concept is extended to entire industries, the results range from the absurd to the near piratical."[27]

The Reagan administration worked to produce an internally
harmonious and inclusive set of tax reforms—another sharp break
from the past. Secretary Regan provided a large measure of protection for tax experts within the Treasury from those congressmen
seeking to expand or protect tax expenditures. Free to dream on

---

[26] Quotation is from Cannon, *President Reagan: The Role of a Lifetime*, 566.

[27] Donald T. Regan, *For the Record: From Wall Street to Washington* (New York: Harcourt Brace Jovanovich, 1988), 207.

paper, the Treasury experts, led by the economic coordinator of the project, C. Eugene Steurerle, Assistant Secretaries for Tax Policy John E. (Buck) Chapoton and Ronald Pearlman, and Deputy Assistant Secretary for Tax Analysis Charles E. McLure, produced a coherent set of proposals known as "Treasury I." These proposals implemented the ideas of Henry Simons, attacked "tax-code socialism" in the form of the investment tax credit and accelerated depreciation write-offs, attempted to index everything for inflation, and pushed to increase corporate taxes.

The proposals in Treasury I included both a dramatic reduction of rates on individual and corporate incomes and the elimination of a wide variety of deductions. For individuals, Treasury I proposed eliminating the deduction of mortgage interest on all but principal residences, drastically limiting the deductibility of consumer interest, eliminating the deduction of charitable contributions except for those who itemized tax returns, and eradicating the deduction of state and local taxes. For corporations, Treasury I would have repealed the investment tax credit, repealed the accelerated deduction of depreciation expenses, removed the deduction for business meals and entertainment, and attacked the oil and gas industry's write-off of intangible drilling costs.

James Baker, the former White House chief of staff who swapped jobs with Donald Regan and became secretary of the treasury in January 1985, stayed on course. Baker and Richard Darman, whom Baker had brought with him to Treasury as assistant secretary, somewhat diluted Treasury I. But they kept its essentials, including the heavier taxation of corporations, in Treasury II and worked to line up extensive support for the package before announcing it, just as they had in their successful effort at Social Security reform in 1983. Darman powerfully reinforced an approach to tax reform that favored entrepreneurship. Also, he believed that providing a greater measure of horizontal equity to the tax system would assist in restoring confidence in government.

President Reagan confidently embraced Treasury II in May 1985 in a nationally televised speech.[28]

Another key difference from earlier episodes of reform then began to emerge. The tax-writing committees of Congress supported the reform process. Democrat Daniel Rostenkowski, chair of the House Ways and Means Committee, became a powerful advocate of the new approach to reform. He did not share Bradley's intellectual enthusiasm for it, but he respected the base-broadening advice he received from the staff of the Joint Committee on Taxation, and he saw ideological merit in joining the movement. He was convinced that the Democrats, as well as the president, had to be visible advocates of reform. He declared, "I'm a Democrat. Reform, fairness—they've all been in the Democratic platform for as long as I've been a Democrat. And I'm not going to let Ronald Reagan get to my left, I'll tell you that much."[29]

Rostenkowski enthusiastically assumed a highly public role, speaking on television for the party in response to the president's May 1985 call for tax reform. More than 75,000 persons answered his call to write "R-O-S-T-Y, Washington, D.C. . . . and stand up for fairness and lower taxes." Afterward, Rostenkowski bragged that "I really took over the [Democratic] party on that 'Write Rosty' speech."[30]

Rostenkowski also worked for reform behind the scenes, countering the lobbyists representing those who would lose from Treasury II. He even enlisted Bill Bradley's help. Bradley met with

---

[28] Assistant Secretary of the Treasury Richard Darman described enterprise-favoring elimination of tax expenditures as "tax populism." See Richard G. Darman, "Populist Force Behind Tax Reform Suggests Future Culture Shifts," *Financier* X (December 1986): 23–32, and "Beyond Tax Populism," *Society* 24 (September/October 1987): 35–8.

[29] Quotation is from Conlan et al., *Taxing Choices*, 89.

[30] Quotation is from Birnbaum and Murray, *Showdown at Gucci Gulch*, 99–100.

the senior members of the House, with almost every Democratic member of Ways and Means, and with many legislators not on the committee, including the liberal Democratic Study Group. While Bradley courted liberal Democrats, Rostenkowski assured lobbyists that the pro-business Senate would defeat any radical House bill. He told conservative Democrats the same thing, pointing out that this would embarrass Reagan and the Republican Party.

Rostenkowski's tenacity, the effective support of Rostenkowski by Ways and Means Committee staff, particularly tax attorney Robert Leonard, and the active lobbying of Republicans by Reagan and Baker combined to bring success: enough bipartisan support for the House to pass a reform bill on December 16, 1985. This bill provided for somewhat greater tax benefits for individuals than had Treasury II—deductibility of mortgage interest for second homes, of up to $20,000 of consumer interest, and of 100 percent of state and local taxes. The House bill compensated for the revenue loss from these deductions by increasing corporate tax rates and the top rates on individuals. But many reformers feared the Republican-controlled Senate Finance Committee would sabotage their plans.

The Senate Finance Committee, however, did not bury reform. In fact, it produced an even more radical version of tax reform, and approved it unanimously. The chair of the Senate Finance Committee, Robert Packwood of Oregon, was crucial in keeping reform alive.

Packwood was an even more bizarre candidate for a leader of tax reform than was Rostenkowski. Since becoming chair of the Finance Committee in 1984, Packwood had shown that he was firmly within a tradition of using the position to provide incentives to private industry and social programs. During the eighteen months before the passage of the Tax Reform Act of 1986, Packwood received almost $1 million from political action committees—more than any other member of Congress. But the president's leadership turned Packwood, who was up for reelection in 1986, into a reformer. He did not want to take the blame for the death of reform.

After long weeks in which it looked like tax reform would in fact perish in the Finance Committee, Packwood adopted a bold, alternative plan suggested by the staff of the Joint Committee on Taxation. Over a "two-pitcher" lunch at a Washington bar, he and a key political staffer concluded that the only way to get a respectable reform bill through the Finance Committee was to lower the top individual income-tax rate below the rate proposed by the House—to drive it down from 38 percent to 25 percent, if possible. "No guts, no glory," is the way Packwood later described his attitude.[31]

Packwood, also like Rostenkowski, discovered Bradley as a valuable ally. Packwood praised Bradley's original bill and made him a committee insider. With Bradley's support, Packwood and his staff drafted a plan that lowered the corporate rate from 36 percent in the House bill to 33 percent and retained only two rates for individuals: 15 percent and 25 percent. The plan proposed abolishing all deductions for mortgage interest, consumer interest, and charitable contributions. Support within the committee grew, and Senate Majority Leader Robert Dole, who had been chair of the Senate Finance Committee until 1984, also signed on. The committee made only a few changes. (The committee increased the highest individual rate to 32 percent and the top corporate rate to 33 percent; it restored certain oil and gas write-offs and protected the ability of banks to deduct for bad-debt reserves; and it added a variety of deductions—those for mortgage interest for first and

---

[31] Quotation is from Birnbaum and Murray, *Showdown at Gucci Gulch,* 208. For a discussion of the intellectual context for Packwood's conversion to reform see Conlan et al., *Taxing Choices,* 163–5, and for a critical assessment of Packwood see Steuerle, *The Tax Decade,* 115–16.

second homes, charitable contributions by those who itemized returns, and state and local income taxes.)

In May 1986, Packwood's bill won unanimous support from the committee. The bipartisan support engineered by Packwood and Bradley moved the bill quickly through the Senate, which adopted it on June 24, 1986. Many lobbyists sought to curry favor with Packwood by supporting the drastic reforms. They hoped to gut the final bill within the conference committee that would reconcile the House and Senate bills.

The two bills contained key elements of agreement. Both bills provided important benefits for lower-income groups through sharp increases in the personal exemption, the standard deduction, and the Earned Income Tax Credit (EITC). The EITC, created as a minor program in 1975, allowed low-income families to count a portion of their income, which declined as their income rose, as a credit against their taxes.

But the bills contained some significant differences, which the conference committee had to iron out. The House bill closed many corporate loopholes but was less aggressive in eliminating the tax preferences used by individuals. In contrast, the Senate bill made sweeping reforms on the individual side of the tax code but left more corporate tax breaks unchallenged. And the top rates on both individuals and corporations were lower in the Senate bill— 32 percent versus 38 percent for individuals and 33 percent versus 36 percent for corporations.

Rostenkowski and Packwood struck much of the final deal in private, removed from the direct pressure of the contending interests. Rostenkowski, impressed by public enthusiasm for lower rates, agreed to accept rates very close to those proposed by the Senate. In the heyday of the era of easy finance, this might have been the final bargain, with each party claiming credit for significant tax reductions. But at this point, the influence of another factor—a critical factor in differentiating the 1986 tax reforms from earlier ones—came decisively into play.

This new factor was the restrictive fiscal and economic environment. Sluggish economic growth, massive deficits, ERTA, and Gramm-Rudman meant that Congress could no longer enact its traditional "reform" bills—ones providing significant tax reductions to particular groups—that reduced the overall level of taxation. Nor could Congress any longer rely on inflation- or growth-driven tax increases to finance tax reductions. Congress had to pay for every reduction in tax rates and every increase in tax loopholes by identifying losers—through a reduction in loopholes elsewhere in the tax code.[32]

In their negotiations, Rostenkowski and Packwood implemented the goal of revenue neutrality. Each of them paid for the rate reductions by sacrificing some of their favorite tax expenditures. Rostenkowski agreed to give up some benefits for individual taxpayers. He agreed to eliminate the deductibility of a variety of items: consumer interest, state and local sales taxes, IRAs for those with pension plans, and charitable contributions for those who did not itemize their deductions. Packwood agreed to cutting an even wider swath through corporate tax preferences. For example, the final bill repealed for the largest banks the deductions they could take for bad-debt reserves and cut back for the biggest oil producers their write-offs of intangible drilling costs. As a consequence of Packwood's going even further in assaulting "tax socialism," the major losers in 1986 were numerous corporations and industries for whom the loss of benefits from the investment

---

[32] For discussions of the influence of the changed fiscal circumstances, see Steuerle, *The Tax Decade,* and "Financing the American State at the Turn of the Century," in Brownlee, ed., *Funding the Modern American State,* 410–45.

tax credit, the preferential taxation of long-term capital gains, and a variety of tax shelters was greater than their gains from the reduction of the top corporate rate from 48 to 34 percent.

In September, the conference committee approved the deal, and President Reagan declared the act "a triumph for the American people and the American system."[33]

In sum, in 1986 a bipartisan group of political entrepreneurs, led by President Reagan and Senator Bradley, had successfully championed an approach to tax reform never previously associated with either of the two major parties: focusing reform of the income tax on broadening its income base and creating a more uniform—a more "horizontally" equitable—tax, even at the expense of sacrificing its progressive rate structure. The resulting legislation—the Tax Reform Act of 1986—was even more consequential than ERTA. The 1986 act amounted to the most dramatic transformation of federal tax policy since World War II. For Senator Bradley and a few other Democratic liberals, the most important thing was that by attacking special deductions and credits, the act moved toward eliminating tax-based privilege and reaffirming the duties of citizenship. For the president and his advisers, the most important aspect of the act was its reduced rate structure and its encouragement of economic enterprise. Leaders of the Reagan administration and Democratic liberals alike welcomed the act's emphasis on broadening the income-tax base. That broadening, along with the reduction in rates, seemed to promote economic efficiency in the face of the sluggish growth of national productivity.

The income tax was in more flux during the 1980s than at any other time since the 1940s. Taxes had turned out to be "up for grabs" to a degree that was surprising to almost all observers. To

---

[33] Quotation is from Birnbaum and Murray, *Showdown at Gucci Gulch,* 283.

some tax experts—those who had championed base-broadening reform—the political flux and the substantive content of the 1986 reforms created new opportunities. Joseph Pechman stressed one of them. In 1989 he estimated that, as a consequence of the 1986 elimination of tax shelters, the adoption of a very modest increase in rates—as little as three percentage points across the board— could raise as much as $100 billion a year. To Pechman and others, the Tax Reform Act of 1986 seemed to open the way for Congress to establish a new tax regime—one based on a reinvigorated income tax.[34]

[34] Joseph Pechman, "More Tax Reform," *Wilson Quarterly* XIII (Summer 1989): 141–2.

4

From 1986 to 1996, and beyond

Nearly ten years have passed since the Tax Reform Act of 1986, but the energized tax regime that Joseph Pechman hoped for has not yet emerged. The potential for a renewal of a tax regime based on income taxation remains unrealized. The key provisions of the 1986 act remain intact, but Congress has not passed any across-the-board rate increases. Nor has it broadened the tax base of income taxation through significant reductions in tax expenditures.

The primary explanation of the lack of progress along the pioneering lines of 1986 is the growth of popular hostility to government. The antigovernment movement that gathered force during the late 1970s and the 1980s has, if anything, waxed stronger in the 1990s. That movement, with its basis in an increasingly alienated middle class, has created growing opposition to either across-the-board tax increases or the elimination of tax expenditures, such as the home-mortgage deduction, that favor large segments of society. The movement has augmented the forces of pluralism, the influence of local and other special interests, and the conflict within a divided government.

Simultaneously, the nation's political leaders have been reluctant to assume the risks required to assemble new coalitions around reform ideas. In the realm of tax policy, politicians have drifted back to the tactics, so popular in 1981 and before, of bidding for support by offering special favors. No significant erosion has occurred in the agreements that produced the Tax Reform Act of 1986, but the shift in tax politics during the decade that followed made substantial tax increases or further base-broadening reforms difficult to achieve.

A DECAYING FISCAL REGIME

In the 1990s, however, even the kind of tax increases proposed by Joseph Pechman might not be sufficient to address the nation's current fiscal needs. Economic conditions are unfavorable for a return to an income-tax regime that would have great revenue elasticity. Even if inflation were to increase, the existing income tax would not be as productive as it was in the era of easy finance, because in 1981 the federal government indexed the income tax for inflation during the years after 1984. Moreover, the nation faces increasing fiscal pressure from what economist Eugene Steuerle calls the "yoke of prior commitments." This is the cost of the many programs, including tax-expenditure programs, that automatically grow more rapidly than does the economy. They relentlessly narrow the discretion available to legislators. The "yoke," along with interest payments on the national debt, has increased budget deficits and will soon exhaust the "peace dividends," which were important to funding new domestic programs after all the major military endeavors prior to the Cold War. Thus even modest increases in income tax rates would be unlikely to throw off the "yoke of prior commitments" and eliminate federal deficits. Almost certainly, such increases would also be unable to fund new domestic programs. In the 1990s it has become impossible to create such programs without further increasing deficit spending.[1]

Even if the federal government did enact tax increases, it would have to reorder its priorities in order to reduce budget deficits or create some fiscal latitude for new domestic or international programs. In particular, it would have to rely to an unprecedented extent on reallocating funds from established domestic programs. But acquiring significant new resources through such reallocations requires the same kind of "identification of losers" that has constrained the politics of raising taxes. To reallocate, the federal government may have to adopt a new set of budget procedures or rules. Such rules would require policymakers to look comprehensively at expenditures and taxation and take into account the total effect on the economy. If effective, this kind of procedural change would be of sufficient scope and influence to define a new fiscal regime. Such a change would constitute a response to Herbert Stein's call, sounded as early as 1970, for the federal government to consider and determine federal fiscal policy with reference not only to budgetary effects—an approach that Stein deems an intellectual failure—but also to the effects on the size and distribution of the nation's economic product.[2]

But it may be that a new fiscal regime is already in place. Perhaps we have already experienced a regime shift with the enormous increase in federal deficits during the 1980s. The new regime

---

[1] Steuerle, "Financing the American State at the Turn of the Century," in Brownlee, ed., *Funding the Modern American State*, 420–1.

[2] For suggestions regarding procedural reform, see Steuerle, "Financing the American State at the Turn of the Century," in Brownlee, ed., *Funding the Modern American State*, 441–4. On Stein's 1970 position, see his "Fiscal Revolution in America, Part II," in Brownlee, ed., *Funding the Modern American State*, 224. For his more recent elaboration, see Stein, *Governing the $5 Trillion Economy* (New York: Oxford University Press, 1989).

would represent an intentional shift in the social contract to impose on future taxpayers a substantially larger share of the costs of domestic programs. In the absence of inflation, deficits now will require higher taxes in the future. Future taxpayers would have no choice in deciding whether or not to shoulder the costs, but they would be able to devise their own tax regime to pay for them. Herbert Stein describes the "Big Budget Bang" in 1981 as just such a policy choice, initiating a new fiscal regime—but postponing the creation of a new tax regime.

A national fiscal regime that depends heavily on deficits would be without precedent in the United States. Its emergence, however, would be understandable historically. Each of the nation's previous fiscal regimes was based primarily on tax increases, and a process of social learning that accompanied the increases, during national emergencies. But fifty years have elapsed since the last emergency. Until the 1980s, massive reliance on deficit spending was limited to the funding of wars. Thus, until the 1980s, taxation—rather than borrowing—lent fiscal regimes their distinctive character. Before then, consequently, the terms "fiscal regime" and "tax regime" could be used interchangeably.

However, if the federal government wishes to reduce significantly its budget deficit and break "the yoke of prior commitments," let alone initiate new domestic programs, it will have to establish a new and different fiscal regime. As the twenty-first century nears, it remains to be seen whether the nation can, for the first time, devise a new regime without first enduring the exigencies of a national emergency.

TOWARD A NEW TAX REGIME?

Policy shifts in the 1980s offered some basis for believing that the nation might embrace a new fiscal regime—one that included breaking "the yoke of prior commitments," broadening the tax base to deal with the tax-entitlement portion of the "yoke," and possibly restructuring taxes themselves. The deficit-reduction measures enacted by Gramm-Rudman-Hollings and subsequent legislation, the Social Security reforms of 1983, and the Tax Reform Act of 1986 (which accepted the principle that tax reductions should be offset by tax increases) all reflected the kind of political leadership and discipline that would be required, on a larger scale, to usher in the new regime.[3]

The late 1980s and early 1990s, however, have not provided comparable examples of leadership. The Reagan administration showed little interest in pressing further for tax reform, perhaps because Secretary of the Treasury Baker feared that so doing would put the 1986 accomplishments at risk.[4] The administration of President George Bush evinced little interest in advancing tax reform along the bipartisan lines laid out in 1986. In fact, his 1988 campaign slogan—"Read my lips: No new taxes!"—may have implied that Bush was running against the 1986 reforms. He seemed to be trying to appeal to the disappointment of middle-class taxpayers who saw little tax relief in the face of increasing economic insecurity. Many middle-class families may have understood that escalating Social Security tax rates effectively canceled out any benefits they received from the income-tax rate cuts that took place during the Carter and Reagan administrations. They may also have understood that during those administrations the changes in the tax code, taken as a whole, had produced virtually no net change in the effective tax rates for any income group.[5]

---

[3] Herbert Stein, however, points out that even in 1994, the makers of fiscal policy still lacked an understanding of the economic consequences of deficits. Such an understanding could contribute to—and might well even be required for—sustained fiscal discipline.

[4] For this interpretation of Secretary Baker, see Steuerle, *The Tax Decade,* 163.

[5] Kevin Phillips, *The Politics of Rich and Poor* (New York: Random House, 1990), 74–91. For a summary of the changes in net tax rates, see Steuerle,

Rather than advancing a program of comprehensive tax reform, the Bush administration turned back toward a more traditional kind of class-oriented tax politics. Bush and his secretary of the Treasury, Nicholas F. Brady, called for substantial cuts in capital-gains taxation. Their strategy backfired. Such proposals had little chance of success in a Democratic Congress and, in fact, opened the door for the congressional leadership to resume the ideologically comfortable position of calling for a return to a higher degree of progressiveness in income taxation. During the 1990 negotiations over the deficit-reduction package in the Omnibus Budget Reconciliation Act of 1990 (OBRA '90), the congressional Democratic leadership was able to force the president to agree to the progressive measures of an increase in the tax rate on the highest incomes and a large augmentation to the Earned Income Tax Credit (EITC). Originally, the EITC meant simply to ease the burden of increased Social Security taxes on the working poor; in its dramatic 1990 expansion, the EITC became welfare reform. It encouraged families dependent on welfare to enter the labor market by cushioning the consequent loss of welfare benefits.[6]

In return for the progressive provisions, a five cents-per-gallon increase in gasoline taxes, and other "revenue enhancements," the

The Tax Decade, 194–6. See also Richard Kasten, Frank Sammartino, and Eric Toder, "Trends in Federal Tax Progressivity, 1980–1993," in Joel Slemrod, *Tax Progressivity and Income Inequality* (Cambridge: Cambridge University Press, 1994), 9–50.

[6] In 1990, for the first time, the EITC provided a rate of credit that was larger than the combined employer and employee Social Security tax rate. For analysis of EITC, see three articles in the *National Tax Journal* 47 (September 1994). These are Anne L. Alstott, "The Earned Income Tax Credit and Some Fundamental Institutional Dilemmas of Tax-Transfer Integration," 609–19; Stacy Dickert et al., "Taxes and the Poor: A Microsimulation Study of Implicit and Explicit Taxes," 621–38; and Janet Holtzblatt et al., "Promoting Work through the EITC," 591–607. See also C. Eugene Steuerle, "The Future of the Earned Income Tax Credit," *Tax Notes* (June 19, June 26, and July 3, 1995).

Democrats accepted substantial budget cuts over a five-year period. The budget agreement—OBRA '90—did reduce the national
budget deficit substantially—by somewhere between one and two
percent of gross national product, but the agreement failed to
provide principled tax reform. Although most of the 1990 tax
increases fell on the wealthy, and OBRA '90 was designed to
attract popular support, Bush's betrayal of his "No new taxes!"
promise handicapped him in his 1992 reelection bid by casting
doubts on his public character.[7]

Presidential candidate Bill Clinton further shifted the consideration of tax policy to a more traditional politics by stressing the
need for a progressive redistribution of taxation. In his "New
Covenant for Economic Change" and "Plan for America's Future," he rejected any major tax reforms or introduction of new
taxes, such as a national sales tax. He proposed, instead, a special
income-tax cut for the middle class and increases in taxes on the
highest incomes. The details of the tax-cut proposal shifted or
remained vague. Clinton himself probably had serious doubts
about the feasibility of the cuts he proposed in the face of budget
deficits.[8]

---

[7] For analysis of the budget compromise of 1990, especially its lack of
coherent principles, see Steuerle, *The Tax Decade*, 163–84.

[8] From the outset of his political career, Clinton had had an interest in
vigorously progressive tax reform, but he moderated his views as governor
and presidential candidate. In 1974, in his campaign for Congress—his first
campaign for higher office—Clinton proposed minimum corporate taxes, a
reduction of tax credits for companies investing overseas, and excess-profits
taxes on "every industry reaping unwarranted profits during inflation." See
Stanley B. Greenberg, *Middle Class Dreams: The Politics and Power of the
New American Majority* (New York: Random House, 1995), 186–8. In my
discussion of the Clinton administration, I rely on Bob Woodward, *The
Agenda: Inside the Clinton White House* (New York: Simon & Schuster,
1994), which focuses on the development of economic policy during the
first year of the Clinton administration, and also on the more general

But Clinton benefited from the impression that George Bush did not comprehend the depth of the economic problems faced by most Americans, and from their sense that government was of little value—and too expensive. During the 1980s, many middle- and low-income people who felt alienated from government came to agree with the pronouncement of the hotel magnate and con- victed tax-evader Leona Helmsley: "We don't pay taxes. Only the little people pay taxes."[9]

During his first year in office, Clinton gradually abandoned the middle-class tax cut as he focused on the need for deficit reduction. In fact, the concern of the Clinton administration for deficit reduc- tion, as well as for energy conservation, led it to advocate a broad- based energy tax championed by Vice President Albert Gore. This was the all-fuels BTU tax, which would have fallen heavily on middle-class consumers. The House narrowly endorsed the BTU tax, although in a drastically modified form as a consequence of lobbying by corporations, such as aluminum manufacturers and airlines, who consumed huge amounts of energy. But opposition within the Senate Finance Committee—including Republicans and a few Democrats, such as John Breaux of Louisiana and David L. Boren of Oklahoma—resulted in the demise of the BTU-tax pro- posal. The final deficit-reduction actions (in OBRA '93) replaced the BTU tax with a modest, 4.3 cents per gallon tax on gasoline, and added two new tax rates on the largest incomes, which Presi- dent Clinton had proposed. Also at the suggestion of the Clinton administration, OBRA '93 provided another substantial increase in the EITC. Clinton stressed the point that tax increases enacted by Congress on families who earned more than $200,000 would raise 80 percent of the new tax revenues imposed.

history of that year, Elizabeth Drew, *On the Edge: The Clinton Presidency* (New York: Simon & Schuster, 1994). For Clinton and middle-class tax cuts, see Woodward, 31 and 42, and Drew, 59–60.

[9] *New York Times,* July 12, 1989.

The Clinton administration, meanwhile, considered how its second priority after deficit reduction—the development of comprehensive health-care reform—might affect the taxes paid by middle-class families. At the outset, Ira Magaziner, Clinton's health-care policy adviser, believed that a substantial tax increase might be necessary, at least in the initial stages of the reform. In February 1993, Daniel Rostenkowski, still the chair of House Ways and Means, told Magaziner, "You guys don't get it; you can't send up another tax." But, a few months later, in April, Magaziner's first formal proposal to the president was for the adoption of national sales taxation, in the form of a value-added tax that would raise $60 billion to $80 billion. Secretary of Health and Human Services Donna Shalala revealed publicly that the administration was considering the proposal.

There was, in fact, some support for value-added taxation within the administration. Treasury Secretary Lloyd Bentsen was interested in the BTU tax in part because it opened the way to adopting a broader-based value-added tax. In February, in an Ohio town meeting, Clinton himself suggested that the value-added tax was "something I think we may well have to look at in the future." But by September, when Hillary Rodham Clinton and Magaziner unveiled their health-care plan, an awareness of the potential political backlash had sunk in. The tax component of the plan consisted only of a new cigarette tax (75 cents per pack) and a 1 percent tax on the incomes of large businesses that would not join the proposed pools of insurance buyers.[10]

While Clinton coped with demands for increases or decreases in specific taxes, he developed no interest in broad-gauged tax reform, including reform that would follow the lines pioneered in the Tax Reform Act of 1986. In fact, Clinton favored the tradi-

---

[10] Woodward, *The Agenda*, 147, 168–9, 294. On support within the administration for value-added taxation, see Drew, *On the Edge*, 71, 85, 194.

tional politics of offering tax benefits to specific interests, groups, and classes, rather than a base-broadening strategy. No enthusiasm for reform emerged from the Department of the Treasury, despite the fact that it was one of the traditional homes of base-broadening expertise within the nation's fiscal policy community. Clinton's first secretary of the treasury, Senator Bentsen from Texas, had little interest in leading base-broadening reform. He had been a reluctant supporter of the 1986 tax reforms, and he had discouraged base-broadening efforts after he became chairman of the Senate Finance Committee in 1991. And Clinton's new National Economic Council, which he hoped would lend greater coherence to his economic program, showed no interest in base-broadening strategies.

Clinton, however, failed to deliver any significant tax cuts for the middle class. This, coupled with his vain effort to enact an ambitious, comprehensive health-care program, made him politically vulnerable. Many middle-class voters saw no improvement in the quality of government, failed to see any significant redistribution of taxes or any increase in tax fairness, and regarded Clinton's deficit reductions as too modest. Some believed that Clinton had betrayed his promise of a middle-class tax cut, and that the president had deliberately misled the public by claiming that an increase in cigarette taxes would be enough to pay for health-care reform. Middle-class rebellion that was focused on issues of taxation may well have contributed significantly to the Republican electoral landslide in 1994 under the "Contract with America" proposed by Congressman Newt Gingrich and his conservative colleagues.

Part of the Contract called for procedural changes designed to eliminate the deficit. In January 1995, the House passed a proposal to amend the Constitution to require a balanced budget by the year 2002. The amendment would require the president to submit a balanced budget and would allow Congress to run a deficit only during wartime or when a three-fifths vote of both the House and the Senate approved the deficit. The assumption was that the amendment, if effective, would force the federal government to live within limited tax revenues and make tough choices among competing programs.

Tax provisions also played a central role in the Republican program. Speaker of the House Gingrich called them the "pièce de résistance" of the Contract with America. In early January 1995 Gingrich and William Archer (R-Texas), the new chair of the House Ways and Means Committee, proposed a set of tax cuts that would benefit middle- and upper-income families. They designed part of the proposals to remind voters of Clinton's aborted middle-class tax cut. Under what Gingrich and Archer called the "American Dream Restoration Act," tax reform would provide a $500 per child tax credit to all taxpaying households earning $200,000 or less, provide a new income-tax credit for two-earner married couples, and exempt from taxation contributions to "American Dream Savings Accounts" (similar to Individual Retirement Accounts) that could be used for certain housing, educational, and medical expenses as well as retirement savings. Archer and Gingrich also advanced measures that more clearly benefited the wealthy. Under the "Job Creation and Wage Enhancement Act," they proposed cutting in half the rates of taxing capital gains, indexing capital gains for inflation, and allowing the deductibility of losses on the sale of principal residences.[11]

The political calculations of Archer and Gingrich seemed to resemble those the Reagan administration had made in 1981. The scale of the suggested tax cuts was substantial (although much

---

[11] Committee on Ways and Means, U.S. House of Representatives, 104th Congress, 1st Session, "Description of Provisions in the Contract with America within the Jurisdiction of the Committee on Ways and Means," January 5, 1995.

smaller than those enacted by ERTA), but Archer and Gingrich proposed no base-broadening and no attempt to make the cuts revenue-neutral. Some Republicans in the House and many in the Senate worried that the tax cuts would put at risk deficit-reduction efforts, which had been successful for three years in a row. Also, they took seriously the advice of economists who told the House Budget Committee that large tax cuts might undermine the successful effort to control inflation. Roger E. Brinner, the chief economist for DRI/McGraw-Hill, described the $500 a child tax credit as "possibly mediocre politics but definitely bad economics."

In early March, the Senate majority leader, Robert Dole, failed to win enough Democratic support to assemble the two-thirds majority required to advance the balanced-budget amendment. By May 1995, the amendment, along with a constitutional amendment to impose congressional term limits, was one of the only two Contract with America provisions that had been voted down in Congress. Republicans, however, made it clear that they would make an issue of the defeat of the balanced-budget amendment in the 1996 general elections.

The defeat augmented Republican concerns over deficits and provided a convenient excuse for leading Republicans to resist the Contract's tax cuts. Before the House voted on the Contract tax package, Senate Republicans on the Finance Committee took the lead in articulating their doubts. Senator Robert Packwood, chair of the Senate Finance Committee, stressed that "reducing the deficit is the most important thing to do." Senator John Chafee (R-Rhode Island), another member of Finance, declared, "Basically, I'm opposed to tax cuts . . . as much as we love to parcel them out." Senator Alfonse D'Amato, also a Finance Committee member, warned that the federal government had to "cut spending and get the deficit under control, that's number one. . . . Otherwise we're going to end up as Mexico II." Enough Republicans in the House worried about the lack of revenue neutrality to slow down passage of the Archer-Gingrich tax cuts. They held up the tax package in the House until Gingrich and Archer agreed to tie their tax-relief legislation to the achievement of future deficit reductions. Many Republicans in the Senate, however, were not satisfied by this stipulation. In late May 1995 enough joined Democrats so that the Senate delivered a resounding defeat to the Contract with America tax legislation.[12]

Meanwhile, both the Senate and the House approved budget resolutions that mapped out plans for balancing the federal budget in seven years. But, in their separate resolutions, the two chambers remained far apart on exactly how they would do the balancing. The gap was largest in the area of taxes, where the House proposed $353 billion in tax cuts over the seven years (following the road map of the Contract with America tax reforms), whereas the Senate put forward a more modest $170 billion. The Senate's cuts would take effect only if lower deficits strengthened the economy and created windfalls for the federal government in the form of lower interest payments and larger tax revenues.[13]

By mid-1995, the Senate had still not formulated its own tax program for fiscal year 1996. Republican leaders in the Senate realized they had to win significant Democratic support to get any tax measure to a vote of the full body. Republicans on the Senate Finance Committee continued to have grave doubts about the political and economic risks of excessive cutting of taxes and government. They preferred to respond to grassroots hostility to taxes with less tax cutting and more tax reform—particularly tax reform that increased horizontal equity and economic efficiency and reduced the costs of government.

[12] Eric Pianin, "Tax Cutters Lose Steam in Senate; House Panel to Unveil GOP Revenue Plan," *Washington Post*, March 14, 1995.

[13] Michael Wines, "Fight Now Turns Intraparty, and Battleground Is Taxes," *New York Times*, May 26, 1995.

To bring about a shift of emphasis from middle-class tax cuts to tax reform, several Republican leaders, supported by a few Democrats, began to propose drastic renovation of the federal tax system. All of the radical proposals had in common the goals of protecting revenues while responding to popular antitax sentiment. The proposals embraced goals of stimulating investment and promoting horizontal equity that had been central to the Tax Reform Act of 1986 but emphasized, as well, the desirability of simplifying the tax system for the taxpayer and reducing the size and power of the enforcement bureaucracy—the Internal Revenue Service (IRS).[14]

Two proposals from within the Senate were similar to ones that had surfaced in earlier periods of fiscal ferment. Senator Sam Nunn (D-Georgia) and Senator Pete Domenici (R-New Mexico), chair of the Senate Budget Committee, put forward the only major bipartisan measure, and the only fully articulated piece of legislation. They called their proposal the Unlimited Savings Allowance tax—the "USA Tax." It was a hybrid of income taxation and consumption taxation.

For individuals, the USA Tax would keep the income tax (including its progressive rates) but eliminate many tax expenditures in return for allowing unlimited deduction for savings, a partial deduction of educational expenses, and a credit for Social Security taxes.

For businesses, the USA Tax would establish an 11 percent value-added tax. By allowing the expensing of investment (the full write-off of investment during the year it is made), the value-added tax would provide major assistance to capital-intensive industries. The USA tax also allowed a dollar-for-dollar credit for Social

---

[14] For a useful introduction to the shape of the radical reform measures, see Peter Passell, "The Tax Code Heads into the Operating Room," and "For Business, the Stakes Are High," *New York Times,* September 3, 1995.

Security payroll taxes. Nunn and Domenici hoped that the latter measure would promote increases in employment.

Overall, the USA Tax proposal was reminiscent of the "spendings" tax suggested by Thomas S. Adams after World War I and favored for a time during World War II by Secretary of the Treasury Morgenthau. Senator Nunn explained that "we are basically going to tax people on what they take out of the economy—above a tax free level for necessities—rather than what they put into the economy by working and saving."[15]

The more radical idea of replacing all of income taxation with a national sales tax, often the favorite conservative alternative to income taxation since World War I, also resurfaced. Senator Richard Lugar (R-Ohio) along with William Archer proposed it. They estimated that a single rate of 16 percent on sales of everything except food and medical services would replace all income-tax revenues. Lugar and Archer hoped to abolish altogether the income tax and the IRS. (The states would collect sales taxes for the federal government.) One House member, Nick Smith of Michigan, found this aspect of the proposal to be its most attractive feature. He welcomed "repeal of the Sixteenth Amendment and dismantling of the Internal Revenue Department" so that "special interests could [not] again come and complicate the existing Tax Code."[16]

A less familiar proposal came from Richard Armey, the Republican majority leader of the House. In June he shifted his attention

---

[15] For discussion of S.722 (USA Tax Act of 1995) by Senators Nunn and Domenici, including a description of the development of the bill over a three-year period, see *Congressional Record* (Senate—April 25, 1995), S5664 ff.

[16] "Just the Job for Jack Kemp," *The Economist,* April 8, 1995; Nick Smith, "Alternatives to Our Current Tax System," *Congressional Record* (House—June 8, 1995), H5704; Carolyn Lochhead, "Elimination of Tax Code Gaining Favor," *San Francisco Chronicle,* July 24, 1995.

from the provisions of the Contract to introduce the "flat tax" in what he called the "Freedom and Fairness Restoration Act (FFRA)."

The "flat tax" in Title I of the FFRA was a proposal that economists Robert Hall and Alvin Rabushka had advanced in the mid-1980s as a replacement for the existing income-tax system. In Armey's version, the tax would require individuals and corporations to pay a flat rate that would decline from 20 percent in the first year to 17 percent in the third year. Individuals would pay taxes only on wages, salaries, and pensions. They would not have the benefit of any deductions. They would, however, have a general personal exemption that would eliminate taxes for a family of four earning less than, roughly, $37,000. Because of the tax's simplicity, individuals supposedly would have to fill out postcard-size forms with only ten lines. The corporate flat-rate payments would include taxes on all other kinds of income, especially interest and dividends, but would allow corporations to deduct their investment in capital equipment, structures, and land from their income (in the year those investments were made) before paying taxes. Corporations would no longer withhold the taxes owed by individual taxpayers. Individuals would write monthly checks to the IRS.

In describing the flat tax, Armey emphasized that it would eliminate the double taxation of dividends under both corporate and personal-income taxation. He claimed it would also promote investment, lose relatively little revenue (about 5 percent per year, according to his estimates), and win popularity because "it combines simplicity and fairness." Jon Fox (R-Pennsylvania) added that the tax would "get the IRS and government off the backs of individual and corporate taxpayers, and will allow all of us to redirect our energies to more productive pursuits." Republican presidential candidates Phil Gramm, Lamar Alexander, and Arlen Specter all joined in proposing variations on the tax. Senator

Specter's included deductions for interest on home mortgages up to $100,000 and for charitable contributions (up to $2,500 per year), and maintained payroll withholding.[17]

To help build a Republican consensus behind an approach to tax reform, Gingrich and Dole announced in early April that they had appointed a commission, chaired by Jack Kemp, to consider a complete overhaul of the federal tax system, including possible repeal of the income tax. Gingrich and Dole asked the nine-member panel to report its recommendations by October 1995. Kemp had withdrawn from the race for the presidency, but he explained that the appointment "puts me back to the center of the debate for the 1996 campaign." Kemp, however, was far from neutral. He was opposed to punishing consumption and advocated a flat tax, which he believed would turn America into "an enterprise zone from sea to shining sea."[18]

Democratic leaders apart from Sam Nunn were slow to develop their own approaches to comprehensive tax reform. They focused, instead, on tax cuts proposed by the Contract for OBRA '95. In February the president countered with his own tax cuts. He also proposed a $500 credit per child and an expansion of the use of IRAs for family expenses like those identified by the Contract, with the addition of long periods of unemployment and the care of an ill parent. He added a tax deduction of up to $10,000 per year for middle-income families to pay for postsecondary education and training. But Clinton's approach would have phased out benefits to families earning more than $60,000. Clinton claimed

---

[17] For descriptions of the flat-tax proposal, see Robert Hall and Alvin Rabushka, *The Flat-Tax,* 2d ed. (Stanford: Hoover Institution Press, 1995), and Dick Armey to the Editor, *New York Times,* April 23, 1995. For supporting comments see, for example, Jon Fox, "The Flat Tax," *Congressional Record* (House—May 10, 1995), H4790.

[18] *New York Times,* April 4, 1995; "Just the Job for Jack Kemp," *The Economist,* April 8, 1995.

that the administration could find enough expenditure cuts in the budget for fiscal 1996 to fund both the tax cut and substantial deficit reduction.[19]

Other Democratic leaders both inside and outside the administration condemned the Contract's program. Congressman Richard Gephardt denounced it as "an affront to fundamental fairness and decency" because it would take "food from the mouths of children and heat from the homes of senior citizens." Vice President Albert Gore called tax legislation passed by the House "Robin Hood in reverse," claiming that too many of the bill's benefits would fall to taxpayers earning $350,000 or more. Secretary of the Treasury Richard Rubin and Alice Rivlin, director of the Office of Management and Budget, denounced the proposed tax cuts as "fiscally irresponsible" and urged Clinton to threaten to veto them.[20]

Clinton, however, did not promise a veto. The new Republican majority and the Clinton administration seemed to be in general agreement that the federal government would have to undertake at least some middle-class tax cuts financed by future reductions in the size of federal programs and institutions. One observer described the Democratic Party under President Clinton as a "kinder, gentler version of the Republican Party."[21]

Meanwhile, support for tax reform seemed to be growing across the political spectrum. Conservative organizations mobilized to inundate Iowa and New Hampshire with literature on the flat tax

---

[19] "Middle-Class Bill of Rights Tax Relief Act of 1995—Message from the President—PM 17," *Congressional Record* (Senate—February 13, 1995), S2566.

[20] Richard Gephardt, "A Victory Party for the Privileged Few," *Congressional Record* (House—March 10, 1995), H2991; Michael Wines, "Gingrich Promises to Tie Tax Relief to Cuts in Deficit," *New York Times,* April 4, 1995.

[21] Felix G. Rohatyn, "What Became of My Democrats?" *New York Times,* March 31, 1995.

and sales tax, and flat-tax supporters established "The Flat Tax Home Page" on the Internet. On the liberal side, the *New York Times* greeted the Kemp commission by editorializing that "the current tax code is maddeningly complex, costly and unfair." The editor called for a new code that would be "simple, pro-growth, and fair."[22]

In July, House Minority Leader Gephardt proposed the first purely Democratic alternative to the Republican proposals for a shift in tax regimes. Gephardt attacked the flat tax as "the largest redistribution of income in the history of the country" and argued that the income tax should be maintained. But, like Armey, he would take more poor families off the income-tax rolls, lower rates dramatically for most people, and pay for both by eliminating deductions. He argued that the simplification would make the IRS "smaller and less expensive." For Americans who no longer had to file a tax return ("the vast majority," according to Gephardt), "the IRS will be reduced to little more than a mailing address." In addition, the changes would "dramatically scale back the 300-billion dollar industry of tax advisers and preparers, and the 4.5 billion hours Americans spend each year to prepare their taxes."

Gephardt's treatment of taxpayers differed in some important ways from Armey's. In contrast with Armey, Gephardt suggested a much lower rate (10 percent) for most taxpayers (75 percent of them, according to his estimates), continuing the deduction for home-mortgage interest, and retaining the Earned Income Tax Credit for the working poor. He also would retain capital-gains taxation for individuals and keep the taxation of interest and dividends under the personal-income tax—as part of a plan to maintain or even increase the progressiveness of the federal tax system. In even sharper contrast with Armey, Gephardt suggested a high degree of progression for rates on the highest-income fami-

---

[22] "Our Maddening Tax System," *New York Times*, April 16, 1995.

lies to pay for these benefits to low- and middle-income taxpayers. On incomes over roughly $32,000 individuals would pay progressive rates rising from 20 percent to 34 percent. And, finally, Gephardt took account of the antigovernment movement by requiring "a national referendum" for Congress to raise tax rates.[23]

In mid-1995, it remains to be seen if President Clinton will follow the example of President Reagan and advocate an ambitious program of coherent tax reform. One option for the president would be to join Republicans in a bipartisan effort to bring about a shift in tax regimes, perhaps adopting a program that would embrace the USA Tax or incorporate elements of both the Armey and Gephardt proposals. The Clinton administration might be able to devise and sell a compromise based on ideas that a new tax regime must retain or increase progressiveness, enhance horizontal equity, and eliminate double-taxation and tax loopholes that violate economic efficiency.

But on only one occasion has the federal government begun the adoption of a new tax regime during a presidential election. That was in 1916, when a major financial crisis, the shadow of war, close cooperation between a Democratic president and a Democratic Congress, and an irresistible insurgency within the Democratic Party launched the modern federal income tax. Eighty years later, the nation faces another array of troubling economic problems while Newt Gingrich, Richard Armey, and their insurgent legions within the House call for reform almost as stridently as Claude Kitchin and his supporters did. But at least two circumstances are very different in 1996. Partisanship divides the executive from the legislative branch, and the economic issues that the

---

[23] Richard A. Gephardt, "A Democratic Plan for America's Economy: Toward a Fairer, Simpler Tax Code," Address, Center for National Policy, July 6, 1995; "Gephardt Has His Own Plan on Tax Reform," *San Francisco Chronicle,* July 7, 1995; William M. Welch, "Gephardt Tax Plan Edges Democrats into Debate," *USA Today,* July 7, 1995.

federal government would have to address in making the transition to a new tax regime are far more complex than they were in 1916. It seems virtually certain that these contingencies mean no dramatic movement toward a new tax regime in 1996 but, instead, a major debate over federal taxation that would extend through the presidential and congressional elections, and beyond. For the moment, the essentials of the tax system introduced during World War II remain in place.

GUIDELINES FROM HISTORY

In the history of federal tax regimes, tax and fiscal reformers in 1996 may find some substantive guidance in designing their reform strategies. The most fundamental fact for reformers to bear in mind is that the introduction of new tax regimes has never stood alone. Every new regime has always been an integral part of a larger transformation of government that, in turn, was bound up in the resolution of a national emergency. As such, each of the new regimes had a reciprocal relationship with the larger transformation of government. On the one hand, the tax regimes enhanced trust in the larger transformation of government. The best example of this was the adoption of highly progressive corporate and individual taxation during World War I. Creating this tax system built public trust in the intervention in World War I, and the mobilization that accompanied it. The tax system of World War II was less progressive but it too helped Americans accept wartime sacrifice. On the other hand, the new tax regimes received support and legitimacy as a consequence of the larger institutional transformation. For example, public confidence in the democratic purposes of American participation in World War I increased support for a new tax regime. More dramatically, the popularity of the massive mobilization for World War II helped win acceptance for the mass-based income tax. In short, all earlier, transforming episodes of fiscal reform have taken place in the context of public trust of the federal government *and* augmented that trust.

If the federal government does fabricate a new, more supple fiscal regime—including both tax reform and breaking the "yoke of prior commitments"—it will do so only if it both recaptures public trust through a larger reconstruction of government and, at the same time, uses the introduction of a new regime as a vehicle to win public trust. Americans must believe that the federal government is working effectively to solve the nation's structural problems—in part through tax reform—before they will be willing to support significant tax increases, embrace new taxes, or accept reductions in the tax benefits they receive from the federal government. Until that trust returns and tax policy contributes to building that trust, special-interest politics will continue to have great force in the shaping of taxation. Both the affluent and middle- and low-income families who are alienated from politics and government will tend to fear that any reform measures—especially the introduction of new taxes that promise to reduce tax burdens—are nothing more than covert devices to increase their taxes or remove their tax benefits.[24]

---

[24] The architects of the Contract with America and the flat tax conceive of their proposed tax reform as a piece of a large pattern of government reform, but theirs is not the only contemporary proposal for a radically new tax regime linked to a much larger agenda. Michael Lind, for example, a defector from the ranks of the neoconservatives, puts ideas for a new tax regime in the center of his program for a "liberal nationalism." His regime would include a substantially more progressive and broad-based income tax to redistribute "the economic gains from automation" and assault the power of what he calls the "overclass" (including the upper middle class), replacement of Social Security payroll taxes with income and consumption taxes, the creation of "social tariffs" to protect high-wage American workers and encourage domestic investment in automation, and the adoption of national standards for property-tax assessment. See Michael Lind, *The Next American Nation* (New York: The Free Press, 1995), 101, 182, 188 ff., 216, 310, 319, 322 ff.

The fiscal history of the federal government suggests that establishing trusted tax regimes—or introducing new tax regimes that enhance confidence in government—has required several key institutional elements. In particular, the successful creation of new tax regimes has included some combination of three elements: (1) enhanced progressiveness in rate structure, (2) allocation of revenues raised by regressive taxes to programs whose benefits are distributed progressively, and (3) regulation of behavior in ways that were widely regarded as improving the national well-being.

The Civil War tax regime, based on high tariffs, incorporated the second and third elements. The second element was financing Civil War pensions and the third was encouragement of a national market in which wages and profits were high. The World War I regime was swept in not only on an ethos of national sacrifice but also on the conviction that government should tax away or deter the accumulation of ill-gotten or socially dangerous assets (e.g., excess profits and incomes, large estates, undistributed profits) and punish "sinful" behavior. The New Deal tax regime encompassed all three elements, and the regime introduced during World War II justified mass-based income taxation in terms of not only sacrifice for national survival but also progressive social justice. Although the Tax Reform Act of 1986 did not necessarily signal a new tax regime, it constituted the most important change in tax policy since World War II, and to a significant extent it represented an effort both to promote horizontal equity and to enhance economic productivity. The success of the Tax Reform Act of 1986 may well have signalled that definitions of fairness that stress horizontal equity had grown in their political appeal during the 1970s and 1980s.

In addition to offering suggestions on the substance of tax policy, the history of the great transformations of American taxation could provide the architects of future tax reform with some lessons regarding the process of reform. On the one hand, the history of taxation in America has been turbulent, ridden with conflict involving the interests of both the state and the modern corporation, and heavily constrained by constitutional rules, institutional habits, and technology. It has always been uncertain in its outcome, and today the future of taxation in America may still be very much "up for grabs." On the other hand, the history of national fiscal crises suggests that the federal government, in league with other powerful interests, has the capacity to produce dramatic, strategic changes in tax policy.

The history of national crises suggests that the cause of tax reform must have effective presidential leadership. As party loyalties and party discipline have waned in significance during the twentieth century, presidential leadership has become more important. Whatever the national objectives might be—promotion of domestic savings (public and private), increase in economic productivity, advance of distributional equity, or growth in jobs—they must be stated with coherence, with a clear sense of internal priorities, and with drama. If taxes are to be increased, the specific purposes of those increases must be identified with clarity and cogent justification, linked to the general purposes of government, and developed through a process of consensus building with outreach to contending groups in civil society. Such consensus building will offer the greatest potential for success by embedding any increases in a reform program that is comprehensive in scope—one that involves a systematic integration of all the modes of federal taxation and expenditure.

Presidents not only must articulate and dramatize goals, they must also lend coherence to the process of legislation. The exigencies of major wars and depressions forced—or enabled—presidents to approach tax reform with a sense of mission and a degree of procedural coherence rarely possible under the American constitutional order. But recent experience suggests that a national emergency is not a necessary condition for coherent reform. De-

spite the absence of an emergency, the Reagan administration
approached tax reform in 1986 with an appreciation of this kind
of coherence.

The history of tax policy during periods of national crisis suggests as well that reformers must be alert to the play of historical
contingency. They must watch, in particular, for the moments in
which key players may be willing to change their minds. Tax
reformers would do well to listen to the advice of Thomas S.
Adams, the most important economist in the Treasury between
1917 and 1933. Although he viewed taxation as heavily shaped
by class politics, he found that on some tax issues, "a majority of
legislators and voters are unaffected and disinterested; they may
cast their votes as a more or less disinterested jury." And "in the
adoption of tax legislation there come zero hours, when the zeal
of the narrowly selfish flags." The challenge that Adams saw was
for experts, and for politicians, to take advantage of such openings. "There are thus many important tax problems," he declared,
"which may be settled on the broad basis of equity and sound
public policy, if one is wise and ingenious enough to find the right
solution."[25]

The most dramatic changes in American tax regimes have occurred when administrations have been able to take advantage of
the opportunities, identified by Adams, for what political scientists
have called "social learning." For dramatic change, administrations must approach tax reform in a comprehensive fashion, articulate the goals of reform in ways that rise above the interests of
particular groups, and organize the process of reform to insulate
experts from political pressure. In the politics of tax reform, con-

---

[25] Thomas Sewell Adams, "Ideals and Idealism in Taxation," presidential
address delivered at the Fortieth Annual Meeting of the American Economic Association, December 27, 1927, *American Economic Review*
XVIII (March 1928): 1–7.

flict has always been severe and the outcome uncertain. But in this turbulence, the most significant transformations of tax policy have been managed by politicians and experts who, despite their immersion in a grinding political process, proved able to define and articulate a transcendent public interest.

Historiography and bibliography

Toward the end of World War I, the Austrian sociologist Rudolf Goldscheid proposed a "fiscal sociology" as a new way to study the public budget. He wanted to analyze the budget as "the skeleton of the state stripped of all misleading ideologies."[1] Goldscheid explained that "nowhere [is] the entirety of any given order of society and economy . . . reflected as clearly [as] in the public household, that the State cannot be very different from its financial system, [and] that every single private household is intimately connected with the State household."[2] Another Austrian scholar,

---

[1] Rudolf Goldscheid, *Staatssozialismus oder Staatskapitalismus* (Vienna, 1917), quoted by Joseph A. Schumpeter, *Die Krise des Steuerstaats,* Zeitfragen aus dem Gebiete der Soziologie (Graz and Leipzig, 1918), translated as Schumpeter, "The Crisis of the Tax State," in Alan T. Peacock et al., *International Economic Papers: Translations Prepared for the International Economic Association,* No. 4 (London: Macmillan, 1954), 5–38.

[2] Rudolf Goldscheid, "Staat, offentlicher Haushalt und Gesellschaft, Wesen und Aufgaben der Finanzwissenschaften vom Standpunkte der Soziologie," *Handbuch der Finanzwissenschaft,* ed. by W. Gerloff and F. Meisel, Vol. 1 (Tübingen, 1925), translated as "A Sociological Approach to Problems of Public Finance," in Richard A. Musgrave and Alan T. Peacock, eds., *Classics in the Theory of Public Finance* (London: Macmillan, 1962), 202–13.

the economist Joseph Schumpeter, seconded Goldscheid's proposal and stressed that the fiscal sociology should have a historical basis. In 1918, Schumpeter declared:

The spirit of a people, its cultural level, its social structure, the deeds its policy may prepare—all this and more is written in its fiscal history, stripped of all phrases. He who knows how to listen to its message here discerns the thunder of world history more clearly than anywhere else.[3]

The severe wartime fiscal crisis and attendant debates over the meaning of the modern state within the ruins of the Austro-Hungarian Empire stimulated Goldscheid and Schumpeter to develop their interest in fiscal sociology, fiscal history, and the history of taxation.

In a similar fashion, the fiscal anguish of the American federal government during the 1980s and 1990s and the related political discourse over the proper role and scope of the national government have prompted some American scholars to reconsider the history of public finance and especially of taxation. From a variety of political perspectives, they have begun to revive tax history in order to understand contemporary policy options and to enrich our knowledge of American society and government.

Professional historians, however, have rarely shared Schumpeter's enthusiasm for the potential for understanding a society through the history of its taxation. They have contributed relatively little to broad-gauged scholarship on the history of American taxation, even during the recent revival of interest in tax history within other disciplines. To be sure, historians have provided some monographic research on specific aspects and periods of tax development, and they have occasionally commented on tax

---

[3] Schumpeter, "The Crisis of the Tax State," 7.

policy while writing on broader or related topics. But historians have left the overarching interpretations and the comprehensive surveys to policy scientists, primarily political scientists and economists. No historian has ever authored an extended history of taxation, or of taxation at the federal level, in America.

The most comprehensive book-length histories of American taxation have been written by members of other disciplines: Roy G. Blakey and Gladys C. Blakey (economists), Randolph E. Paul (an attorney), Sidney Ratner (an economist), Edwin R. A. Seligman (an economist), Frank W. Taussig (an economist), and John Witte (a political scientist). Their books, in part because of the paucity of historical scholarship, remain valuable to the contemporary student. Sidney Ratner's *American Taxation: Its History as a Social Force in Democracy* (1942) is still the best single volume on the history of federal taxation through the adoption of mass-based income taxation during World War II. He somewhat updated the book twenty-five years later, in *Taxation and Democracy in America* (1967).[4]

The other general histories provide useful supplements to Ratner's survey. The many editions of Taussig's *The Tariff History of the United States* placed Taussig in a class by himself as a historian of the tariff system, where he remains today, two generations later. His general conclusion that American tariffs, however distasteful in theory, had only limited effects on the domestic economy remains the conventional scholarly wisdom.[5] Edwin Seligman made a variety of contributions to the history of taxation, but most notable was his *The Income Tax: A Study of the History, Theory*

---

[4] See Ratner, *American Taxation: Its History as a Social Force in Democracy* (New York: W. W. Norton, 1942) and *Taxation and Democracy in America* (New York: W. W. Norton, 1967).

[5] The last edition was Taussig, *The Tariff History of the United States: The Eighth Revised Edition* (New York: G. P. Putnam's Sons, 1931).

and Practice of Income Taxation at Home and Abroad (1914), which is the best history of American income taxation, including its European background, prior to World War I.[6] The Blakeys, in *The Federal Income Tax* (1940), amplify Ratner's scholarship, particularly with regard to the development of the federal income tax during World War I and the 1920s.[7] The most informative overview of the articulation of mass-based income taxation during the 1940s and 1950s is Randolph Paul's *Taxation in the United States* (1954), even though Paul, who was a central participant in crafting the World War II tax legislation, did not document his history with footnotes.[8] John Witte's *The Politics and Development of the Federal Income Tax* (1985) provides the most detailed survey of federal tax policy from the 1960s through the early 1980s.[9]

With the exception of John Witte, all of these scholars wrote within a "progressive" intellectual framework. Sidney Ratner articulated the approach most clearly. He argued that the main theme of public finance and tax history during the twentieth century was the struggle between "the thrust for social justice and the counter-thrust for private gain." In 1942, when Ratner's book appeared, the New Deal seemed to have established a clear victory for social justice by having secured progressive income taxation, which Ratner described "as preeminently fit for achieving and

---

[6] See Seligman, *The Income Tax: A Study of the History, Theory and Practice of Income Taxation at Home and Abroad* (New York: Macmillan, 1914). For his contributions to the history of other aspects of taxation, including property and corporate taxation, see Seligman, *Essays in Taxation*, 9th ed. (New York: Macmillan, 1921).

[7] Blakey and Blakey, *The Federal Income Tax* (London: Longmans, Green, 1940).

[8] See Paul, *Taxation in the United States* (Boston: Little, Brown, 1954).

[9] See Witte, *The Politics and Development of the Federal Income Tax* (Madison: University of Wisconsin Press, 1985).

preserving the economic objectives of a democracy." Moreover, the adoption and expansion of income taxation appeared to have created the basis for a well-funded welfare state and for a federal government that could defend the cause of democracy around the world. Ratner's interpretation of tax history was an expression of a larger progressive view of the history of government and reform during the twentieth century. That view regarded the reform movements that culminated in the New Deal as an expression of social democracy and as a stream of victories for working people—farmers and factory laborers.[10]

THE POSTPROGRESSIVE ANALYSIS
OF SOCIAL INTERESTS

The political scientists and economists who have recently explored the history of the federal tax system have dramatically challenged the "progressive history" of income taxation. They have done so by focusing on the question of "who or whose interest it is that sets the machine of the state in motion and speaks through it," to use Schumpeter's words yet again. In the process, they have produced a rich menu of descriptions of the configuration of the "interests" shaping tax policy.[11]

Scholars who have challenged a progressive interpretation of social interests include, among others, neoconservative economists searching for historical foundations for the Reagan "revolution" and its attack on government. They have presented the history of taxation in the twentieth century not as a victory for principled forces of democracy but as the capture of "the state" by narrowly self-interested groups of "tax-eaters." Central to this neoconserva-

---

[10] Ratner, *American Taxation* and *Taxation and Democracy,* 14 and 16 in both editions.

[11] Schumpeter, "The Crisis of the Tax State," 19, n. 19.

tive story is the adoption and expansion of the federal income tax. Ben Baack and Edward J. Ray, in an important article, argue that "the current issue of the impact of special-interest politics on our national well-being has its roots in the bias of discretionary federal spending at the turn of the century" and in the enactment of the federal income tax. They claim that the passage of the Sixteenth Amendment, which authorized income taxation, was intended to raise significant new revenues and was a result of special-interest groups that sought greatly expanded funding for military and social-welfare programs.[12] The most comprehensive statement of a neoconservative interpretation of the expansion of the public sector is the book by economist and economic historian Robert Higgs, *Crisis and Leviathan: Critical Episodes in the Growth of American Government* (1987). Higgs sees the passage of the Sixteenth Amendment as the thin edge of the wedge for interest groups who wanted to use government to redistribute income in their direction, largely by funding their favorite programs.[13]

The progressive and the neoconservative interpretations, despite their differences in identifying and characterizing socially powerful interests, agree that the federal income tax significantly enhanced the power of the state. But most recent scholars of tax history, when tracking group and class influence, have started from quite a different point. Rather than seeking to explain the rise of Leviathan, they have emphasized and tried to understand the weaknesses of the modern federal government.

In so doing, the analysts of weakness have begun by noting three seemingly interrelated fiscal characteristics. The first is the

---

[12] Ben Baack and Edward J. Ray, "The Political Economy of the Origin and Development of the Federal Income Tax," in Robert Higgs, ed., *Emergence of the Modern Political Economy: Research in Economic History* (Supplement 4) (Greenwich, Conn.: JAI Press, 1985), 121–38.

[13] See Higgs, *Crisis and Leviathan: Critical Episodes in the Growth of American Government* (New York: Oxford University Press, 1987).

relatively small size of American tax revenues as a percentage of national income, when compared with tax revenues in Western Europe over much of the post-1941 tax regime. The second is the Swiss-cheese quality of the progressive income tax, a characteristic created by preferential rates of taxation and by tax expenditures. The third is the federal government's huge budget deficit, which has grown in absolute size in most years since 1980. Many scholars regard the deficit as a reflection of both a weak tax-state and a national civic decline.

In the process of identifying these characteristics, a few analysts of weakness have written innovative histories of the international development of twentieth-century institutions of public finance, including those in the United States. Two examples are Sven Steinmo, *Taxation and Democracy: Swedish, British and American Approaches to Financing the Modern State* (1993), and Carolyn Webber and Aaron Wildavsky, *A History of Taxation and Expenditure in the Western World* (1986).[14]

The scholars who explore the weakness of the American tax-state have developed two very different analytical approaches, but

[14] Steinmo, *Taxation and Democracy: Swedish, British and American Approaches to Financing the Modern State* (New Haven: Yale University Press, 1993), and Webber and Wildavsky, *A History of Taxation and Expenditure in the Western World* (New York: Simon & Schuster, 1986). Two excellent international comparative histories do not encompass the United States but focus rather on Europe from the early modern era through the industrial revolution. See Gabriel Ardant, "Financial Policy and Economic Infrastructure of Modern States and Nations," in Charles Tilly, ed., *The Formation of National States in Western Europe* (Princeton: Princeton University Press, 1975), 164–242; and D. E. Schremmer, "Taxation and Public Finance: Britain, France, and Germany," in Peter Mathias and Sidney Pollard, eds., *The Cambridge Economic History of Europe, Volume 8, The Industrial Economies: The Development of Economic and Social Policies* (Cambridge: Cambridge University Press, 1989), 315–494.

both of the approaches are based on the analysis of what Schumpeter called "social power relations."

The first group of scholars who focus on governmental weakness works within a tradition of fiscal analysis that extends back to Rudolf Goldscheid. His central conclusion was that class politics had impoverished the state. Capitalism, he argued, had emasculated feudal states, which he believed had often possessed great fiscal power because of the assets they owned. "The rising bourgeois classes," Goldscheid argued, "wanted a poor State, a State depending for its revenue on their good graces, because these classes knew their own power to depend upon what the State did or did not have money for." So the capitalists "conquered the State by stripping it of its wealth" and created a "tax State," which was dependent on taxing or begging from the very capitalists who controlled the state. The capitalists used its fiscal instruments only when necessary "to enhance their profits and extend their power."[15]

Modern "capitalist-state" theorists follow the general thrust of Goldscheid's interpretation as they attempt to understand what they regard as the failures of the American state to adopt significant programs of social investment or progressive wealth redistribution. These scholars, primarily political scientists, accent the influence of the leadership of the corporate sector and argue that in the nineteenth century, large corporations and the wealthiest Americans captured federal fiscal policy in order to protect the investment system—and their own power. As a consequence, these scholars argue, the federal government abstained from redistributing wealth in a progressive fashion and, instead, reinforced the process of capital accumulation. In so doing, the capitalist-state theorists argue, American government had to wrestle with an inherent dilemma created by democratic political institutions:

---

[15] Goldscheid, "A Sociological Approach," 203, 205, 209, and 211.

How could it respond to democratic pressures for redistributional equity while maximizing capital accumulation?

Prominent among the capitalist-state theorists who focus on fiscal history is the historian and political scientist Robert Stanley, who describes the early history of the federal income tax, from the Civil War through 1913, in *Dimensions of Law in the Service of Order: Origins of the Federal Income Tax, 1861–1913* (1993). He sees the passage of the Civil War law, the enactment of the Sixteenth Amendment, and the reenactment of a federal income tax in 1913 as an expression of capitalist desire "to preserve imbalances in the structure of wealth and opportunity, rather than to ameliorate or abolish them, by strengthening the status quo against the more radical attacks on that structure by the political left and right."[16] Consistent with Stanley's history of the income tax is a history of New Deal tax reform, *The Limits of Symbolic Reform: The New Deal and Taxation* (1984), written by historian Mark Leff, who argues that Franklin D. Roosevelt looked only for symbolic victories in tax reform and was never willing to confront capitalist power by undertaking a serious program of income and wealth redistribution or by significantly expanding taxation of the incomes of upper-middle-class Americans. Thus Stanley and Leff regard income-tax initiatives before World War II as hollow, primarily symbolic efforts to appease the forces of democracy.[17]

The political scientist Ronald King has also advanced an elaborate expression of the capitalist-state approach to fiscal history, in *Money, Time and Politics: Investment Tax Subsidies and American Democracy* (1993). King carries the story told by Stanley and

---

[16] See Stanley, *Dimensions of Law in the Service of Order: Origins of the Federal Income Tax, 1861–1913* (New York: Oxford University Press, 1993), viii–ix.

[17] See Leff, *The Limits of Symbolic Reform: The New Deal and Taxation* (Cambridge: Cambridge University Press, 1984).

Leff into the post–World War II era, in which income-tax revenues came mainly from wages and salaries rather than profits, dividends, and rents, as had been the case earlier. He puts less emphasis on the symbolic use of the language of progressive redistribution to appease democratic forces. Instead, he stresses the role of a "hegemonic tax logic," based on the needs of American capitalism, which first appeared during the 1920s but prevailed only after World War II. This logic, King argues, called for the federal government to adopt tax policies that promoted capital accumulation but at the same time to trumpet them as measures that increased productivity, average wages, and jobs. He argues that all of the presidents after World War II invoked this logic in devising their tax programs. But he finds the administration of John F. Kennedy to have been the most creative in mobilizing investment tax subsidies to accommodate the potentially conflicting interests of business and labor. Kennedy's was, therefore, according to King, "the quintessential presidency of the postwar American regime." Thus, in King's formulation, the loopholes in the federal tax code become more than "random loopholes drilled primarily to satisfy the demands of selfish factions." King argues that the loopholes "reflect a more conscious intention consistent with systematic policy purpose."[18]

The second approach used to explain the fiscal weakness of the modern American state is that of scholars who have described themselves, in various ways, as "pluralists" because they emphasize the multiplicity of contending groups shaping tax policy, and because they detail the ways in which the American political sys-

---

[18] See King, *Money, Time and Politics: Investment Tax Subsidies and American Democracy* (New Haven: Yale University Press, 1993), 37 and 316, and his essay, "From Redistributive to Hegemonic Logic: The Transformation of American Tax Politics, 1894–1963," *Politics and Society* 12 (No. 1, 1983): 1–52.

tem encourages fragmentation of the polity into local and special interests. Whereas the capitalist-state theorists tend to consider tax policy as rationally advancing the interests of capitalists, the pluralists who have written at length about fiscal history stress the economically dysfunctional character of federal tax policy, especially the complex webs of special tax rates and tax expenditures. In this pluralist view, the federal tax code often distorts economic decisions and weakens the federal government by undermining the income-tax base. The political scientist John Witte has written the most comprehensive pluralist history of the income tax, *The Politics and Development of the Federal Income Tax.* In it, he describes the tax system as one of "enormous complexity, which may have reached the limits of legitimacy, the capacity to meet revenue demands, and the capability of reform." The economist Charles Gilbert, in his *American Financing of World War I* (1970), rendered a similar verdict on American tax policy during the First World War.[19]

For the sake of clarity, it should be emphasized that this description of pluralist scholarship as rendering negative judgments of the political process applies only to those pluralist scholars who have written extensive fiscal histories. Other scholars have described politics as pluralist but have rendered much more favorable judgments. But virtually none of the pluralists with more favorable normative evaluations have made substantial contributions to fiscal history.[20]

---

[19] John Witte, *The Politics and Development of the Federal Income Tax* (Madison: University of Wisconsin Press, 1985), 23; Charles Gilbert, *American Financing of World War I* (Westport, Conn.: Greenwood Press, 1970).

[20] Robert A. Dahl and Samuel P. Hays are two of the most obvious examples of more optimistic pluralists. See Dahl, *Democracy and Its Critics* (New Haven: Yale University Press, 1969), and Hays, *The Response to Industrialism, 1885–1914* (Chicago: University of Chicago Press, 1957).

The pluralist analysis of "social power relations" also contrasts sharply with that of the capitalist-state theorists. Pluralists emphasize the extent to which a broad range of middle-class groups has prevailed in the political process. Thus the political scientists Carolyn Webber and Aaron Wildavsky, in *A History of Taxation and Expenditure in the Western World* (1986), wrote: "As Pogo might have put it, we—the broad middle and lower classes—have met the special interests, and 'they is us.' " The outcome, in the words of John Witte, is a system that "essentially exempts the poor, taxes the broad middle class at a very stable rate, and taxes the rich at varying rates depending on political and ideological shifts." Influential political scientists who have analyzed the history of America's Social Security system, including its financing, have reached similar conclusions about the distribution of power. The leading examples of this scholarship include Martha Derthick, *Policymaking for Social Security* (1979), and Carolyn L. Weaver, *The Crisis in Social Security: Economic and Political Origins* (1982).[21]

The pluralist interpretation of the tax-state as historically weakened by the grinding of middle-class interest groups has, in turn, influenced public discourse through "declinists." These are scholars such as historian Paul Kennedy, in *The Rise and Fall of the Great Powers: Economic and Military Conflict from 1500 to 2000* (1988), and the political scientist David Calleo, in *Beyond American Hegemony: The Future of the Western Alliance* (1987) and *The Bankrupting of America: How the Federal Budget Is Impoverishing the Nation* (1992), who bemoan the decline in civic culture

---

[21] Webber and Wildavsky, *A History of Taxation and Expenditure*, 531; Witte, *The Politics and Development of the Federal Income Tax*, 21; Martha Derthick, *Policymaking for Social Security* (Washington, D.C.: Brookings Institution, 1979); and Carolyn L. Weaver, *The Crisis in Social Security: Economic and Political Origins* (Durham, N.C.: Duke University Press, 1982).

in America and regard the great size of federal budget deficits as a symptom of that decline. They have blamed the massive deficits on the failure to raise sufficient tax revenues and, in turn, on middle-class preferences for lower taxes, especially taxes that subsidize middle-class consumption patterns over public social investment. Calleo diagnosed America's economic troubles as in large part the price paid for democratic tax politics. He implied that significant reform of the public sector can come only if the process of tax politics is first reformed—by insulating the tax system from democratic politics.[22]

Thus political scientists and economists have dramatically reinterpreted the forces of democracy lauded by Sidney Ratner. Within the new tax history, democracy has been subverted by narrowly selfish tax-eaters (the neoconservative interpretation) or captured by capitalists or their agents (the capitalist-state view) or transmogrified by the excessive grind of competitive interest groups (the pluralist analysis).

POSTPROGRESSIVE VIEWS OF THE ROLE OF THE STATE

Each of the major postprogressive interpretations of American tax history is "society centered" rather than "state centered." That is to say, in explaining the development of the federal government and its fiscal policies, each attaches greater importance to the influence of interests outside the government than to the role of interests within it.

---

[22] See Kennedy, *The Rise and Fall of the Great Powers: Economic and Military Conflict from 1500 to 2000* (New York: Random House, 1988), especially 434, 527, and 534–5; and Calleo, *Beyond American Hegemony: The Future of the Western Alliance* (New York: Basic Books, 1987), especially 109–13 and 126, and *The Bankrupting of America: How the Federal Budget Is Impoverishing the Nation* (New York: Morrow, 1992).

At the same time, however, the neoconservative, capitalist-state, and pluralist interpretations all pay close attention methodologically to the role of the state; each has a more clearly articulated vision of the role of the state than did the progressive histories. Even the pluralist interpretation, which dwells on the weakness of the state, theoretically defines the role of the state. And both the neoconservative and the capitalist-state arguments accord a degree of autonomy to institutions and actors within the government.

The neoconservative fiscal story offers little detailed analysis of the institutions of the federal government, but in the story, the federal government acquired considerable autonomy during the course of the twentieth century. In particular, neoconservative scholars highlight the success of the federal government in manipulating politics to undermine traditional American resistance to taxpaying, particularly during the New Deal and World War I. Neoconservative scholars feature agents of the state who gain control of the instruments of national communication, manipulate federal power to discourage or suppress grassroots challenges to the state, and cultivate a class of experts capable of designing taxes whose effects are difficult to detect. The historian David Beito, for example, in *Tax Payers in Revolt: Tax Resistance during the Great Depression* (1989), emphasizes the power of a tax-resistant culture that, he claims, dates back to John C. Calhoun. Beito argues that this culture was vital at the state and local levels as late as the 1930s and claims that the New Deal played a crucial role in breaking its back.

The result, the neoconservatives argue, is government growth that impairs productivity—growth fueled both by interest-group politics and self-interested, relatively autonomous agents of the state. In a sense, they echo one of Schumpeter's warnings about the growth of social programs: "If the finances have created and partly formed the modern state, so now the state on its part forms them and enlarges them—deep into the flesh of the private economy." Neoconservative scholars emphasize the need to limit state autonomy in order to restore the health of the republic, and they offer historical evidence to support political movements designed to impose new constitutional restraints, such as balanced-budget amendments and Proposition 13–style limits on tax rates.[23]

For their part, capitalist-state theorists of fiscal policy have moved beyond simplistic models of state capture to express an appreciation for the complexity of the relationship between political leaders and capitalists and for the extent to which the former can acquire autonomy and exercise initiative in establishing policy. Robert Stanley, for example, argues that "political officials" were far more than tools of the capitalists. They acted "as relatively autonomous trustees . . . through the use of multiple dimensions of the law." Thus, Stanley sets the history of early income taxation in what he calls an "omnipresent legal environment" and explores "the full network of lawmaking agencies in their symbiosis with other dimensions of the social structure." Legislatures and courts were aware of the "crucial rhetorical consequences" and the distributional implications of tax law and used their autonomy, through the law, Stanley proposes, to shape popular values and beliefs. He attributes overwhelming responsibility for the enactment of income taxes during the Civil War, in 1894, and again in 1913 to the initiative of the capitalists' "trustees," who he believes acted to preempt the adoption of more radical measures. And he views the fight over the constitutionality of income taxation not as a confrontation between classes but as an argument within the state for control over "centrist" mechanisms of allocation. Thus, Stanley interprets *Pollock v. Farmers' Loan and Trust Co.* (1895), which invalidated the 1894 income tax, as a Jacksonian attack by

---

[23] See Beito, *Tax Payers in Revolt: Tax Resistance during the Great Depression* (Chapel Hill: University of North Carolina Press, 1989); and Schumpeter, "The Crisis of the Tax State," 19.

the Supreme Court on the dominant role of Congress in "statist capitalism" rather than as an assault on income taxation.[24]

Ronald King also finds considerable state autonomy, based on the responsibility of political leaders to reconcile the interests of contending groups and classes. It was by working effectively under this responsibility, King argues, that the architects of the post–World War II tax regime took into account the interests of labor—as well as their own fundamental devotion to capital accumulation—and replaced the "zero-sum redistribution game" with "the politics of non-zero-sum productivity" and a tax policy of economic "growthmanship." By manipulating both tax policy and tax symbolism, state managers induced labor to reduce its pressure for short-run economic and fiscal gains in favor of long-run gains "within overall capitalist hegemony."[25]

In contrast, the federal government portrayed in the pluralist histories of public finance is one of pathetic weakness. Pluralists complement their stress on the power of middle-class interests with a view of the American state as so fragmented that it cannot stand up to the grinding of interest-group competition. The weak political structures cited by the pluralist scholars of tax history include fragmented political parties, a decline of partisanship after World War II, a system of federalism that reinforces local interests, a bureaucracy paralyzed by multiple decision points, and a federal government constitutionally fractured along the legislative-executive fault line. The pluralists argue that these structural weaknesses, combined with a high degree of democratic access to government and with a tax system that encompasses virtually all households and businesses, will necessarily produce an inefficient tax policy that is an incoherent jumble of complexity and that

---

[24] Stanley, *Dimensions of Law*, especially vi–x, 3–14, and 136–75.
[25] See King, *Money, Time and Politics*, 47–85, for the core of his theoretical argument.

fails to raise adequate revenue. And because of these structural weaknesses, those who would reform public finance are condemned to a frustrating process of slow and incremental change.

The most important recent expression of the pluralist understanding of the role of the state in tax policy comes from a political scientist, Sven Steinmo, in *Taxation and Democracy: Swedish, British and American Approaches to Financing the Modern State* (1993). Steinmo concluded that a "fragmentation of political authority"—checks and balances and the localism encouraged by American federalism—strengthens special-interest groups at the expense of political parties and frustrates tax reformers who would broaden the income-tax base or adopt national consumption taxes in order to expand social programs. The fragmentation encourages groups to be exceptionally hostile to any increase in their tax burdens. Steinmo's invocation of comparative analysis and the framework of political science's "new institutionalism" has sharpened the pluralist analysis of the development of American taxation.[26]

THE DEMOCRATIC-INSTITUTIONALIST APPROACH

This book and its companion volume, *Funding the Modern American State, 1941–1995: The Rise and Fall of the Era of Easy Finance* (1995), represent efforts to organize an approach that differs significantly from the pluralist, capitalist-state, and neocon-

---

[26] See Steinmo, *Taxation and Democracy*. For a description of the "new institutionalism," which attempts to embrace the full range of institutional factors in comprehensive models of public-sector development, see James G. March and Johan P. Olsen, *Rediscovering Institutions: The Organizational Basis of Politics* (New York: The Free Press, 1989).

servative approaches to the history of taxation. This new interpretation might be described as "democratic institutionalist."[27]

In its "democratic" dimension, this approach recognizes the power of democratic forces outside the federal government. These were forces that contributed, for example, to the progressively redistributional cast of the twentieth-century tax regimes. At the same time, the interpretation stresses the potency of ideas as independent creative forces. Thus concepts of progressive equity, often expressed as the criterion of the "ability to pay" taxes, shaped and gave intention to democratic pressures. In recognizing the power of democratic forces and ideas of equity, this approach has much in common with older progressive histories.

Democratic institutionalism breaks with progressive history in three important ways. First, the "institutionalist" dimension of this interpretation accents the influence of governmental institutions—particularly the presidency and congressional leadership, professional experts within government, political partisanship, and constitutional structures—in shaping policy. Within these governmental institutions, ideas figure centrally in a process of social learning. Presidents and other policy entrepreneurs, including professional experts, use ideas to understand social change. Moreover, they invoke those ideas to form alliances beyond the formal boundaries of government. Building those alliances, in turn, often encourages the development of supportive policy communities.

The second break with progressive history by scholars of taxation who adopt a democratic institutionalist model is an emphasis on historical contingency, rather than a relentless advance of de-

---

[27] See W. Elliot Brownlee, ed., *Funding the Modern American State, 1941–1995: The Rise and Fall of the Era of Easy Finance* (Washington, D.C.: Woodrow Wilson Center Press; Cambridge: Cambridge University Press, 1995).

mocracy. Most important, the approach suggests that national emergencies have heavily influenced the specific ways in which ideas, democratic forces, and policy networks have interacted to shape important changes in fiscal institutions. In each of the great modern wars, for example, presidents employed tax reforms and invoked democratic ideals of taxation to mobilize the economy, to win support for their administrations, and to unify the nation behind the war effort. The approach also stresses the idea that the transitions between regimes have been heavily "path dependent." In other words, the tax regime imposed in each emergency changed economic, political, and intellectual conditions in ways that made it difficult or even impossible for the federal government to return to the tax regime in force before the emergency. Consequently, today's tax system has a stratified quality. Each layer of tax institutions, almost like a layer of the earth's crust, represents the legacy of an earlier epoch, or fiscal regime.[28]

The third break is an emphasis on how economic development

---

[28] While the democratic-institutionalist interpretation of both state and society differs substantially from the neoconservative, one important neoconservative scholar also stresses the importance of national crises and path dependency to institutional development. See Higgs, *Crisis and Leviathan*, especially 3–74. The first, and most influential, work of historical scholarship to focus attention on the upward-ratchet effect of wars on public expenditures in industrial democracies was Alan T. Peacock and Jack Wiseman, *The Growth of Public Expenditure in the United Kingdom* (Princeton: Princeton University Press, 1961). The leading theorist of the influence of path dependency on historical change is economic historian Paul David. See, for example, Paul David, "Clio and the Economics of QWERTY," *American Economic Association Papers and Proceedings* 75 (May 1985): 332–7, and "Path-Dependence and Predictability in Stochastic Systems with Network Externalities: A Paradigm for Historical Economics," in Dominique Foray and Christoper Freeman, eds., *Technology and the Wealth of Nations* (New York: St. Martin's Press, 1993).

shaped the organizational options available to the architects of tax policy. The democratic-institutional approach attempts to assess how, over time, the changing condition of economic structure and organization has defined the institutional possibilities for the expression of democratic ideals. For example, the interpretation recognizes that the federal government could not embody the ideal of "ability to pay" in its modern form until economic development created the administrative underpinnings for an effective income tax. More generally, economic development, defined to include the emergence and refinement of modern technology and organizational structures as well as economic growth, shapes the public-finance options available to policymakers.[29]

A significant collection of monographic scholarship on the history of taxation could be described as democratic institutionalist, although the scholars do not use that term. Some of this scholarship addresses the origins of the federal tax system during the early republic. Most important, Robert A. Becker, in *Revolution, Reform, and the Politics of American Taxation, 1763–1783* (1980), Roger H. Brown, in *Redeeming the Republic: Federalists, Taxation, and the Origins of the Constitution* (1993), E. James Ferguson, in *The Power of the Purse: A History of American Public Finance, 1776–1790* (1961), and Thomas P. Slaughter, in *The Whiskey Rebellion: Frontier Epilogue to the American Revolution* (1986), all emphasize the role of democratic forces,

---

[29] Public-finance economist Richard Musgrave has led his profession in thinking about the relationship between structural economic change and the development of fiscal regimes. He has proposed an even stronger view of the relationship than the one suggested here. He argues that structural change in highly developed economies has, in fact, driven dramatic changes in tax structure, which he claims would have occurred even without major wars. See Richard A. Musgrave, *Fiscal Systems* (New Haven: Yale University Press, 1969), 125–206.

concepts of equity, and historical contingency in the development of the federal government's first tax regime.[30]

Other specialized scholarship reinforces a democratic-institutionalist interpretation of tax reform by pointing to the importance of democratic forces during the post–Civil War industrial era. Some monographs have suggested the strength of the appeal of the single-tax movement to Americans and its great influence on the mainstream of tax reform, although most scholars of tax history, including those writing from a progressive point of view, have discounted its role. Notable are Charles Barker's biography *Henry George* (1955) and two histories of the movement: the historian Arthur Dudden's *Joseph Fels and the Single-Tax Movement* (1971) and the economist Arthur Young's *The Single Tax Movement in the United States* (1916).[31] In an influential article written more than fifty years ago, Elmer Ellis provided evidence that buttressed Sidney Ratner's emphasis on the role of farmers in shaping the inception of the federal income tax.[32]

The development of federal taxation must be understood in the context of the history of taxation at all levels of government, and

[30] Robert A. Becker, *Revolution, Reform, and the Politics of American Taxation, 1763–1783* (Baton Rouge: Louisiana State University Press, 1980); Roger H. Brown, *Redeeming the Republic: Federalists, Taxation, and the Origins of the Constitution* (Baltimore: Johns Hopkins University Press, 1993); E. James Ferguson, *The Power of the Purse: A History of American Public Finance, 1776–1790* (Chapel Hill: University of North Carolina Press, 1961); and Thomas P. Slaughter, *The Whiskey Rebellion: Frontier Epilogue to the American Revolution* (New York: Oxford University Press, 1986).

[31] Charles A. Barker, *Henry George* (New York: Oxford University Press, 1955); Arthur P. Dudden, *Joseph Fels and the Single-Tax Movement* (Philadelphia: Temple University Press, 1971), 199–245; and Arthur N. Young, *The Single Tax Movement in the United States* (Princeton: Princeton University Press, 1916).

[32] Elmer Ellis, "Public Opinion and the Income Tax, 1860–1900," *Mississippi Valley Historical Review* 27 (September 1940): 225–42.

the histories of taxation at the state and local levels—albeit few and far between—tend to support a democratic-institutionalist interpretation. A number of studies have illustrated how small-property owners—both farmers and middle-class people in towns and cities—pushed for the adoption of new, more progressive taxes at the state and local levels and then supported the adoption of income taxation at the federal level. W. Elliot Brownlee, in *Progressivism and Economic Growth: The Wisconsin Income Tax, 1911–1929* (1974), found the impetus for the adoption of income taxation in Wisconsin to be primarily agrarian. David P. Thelen, in *The New Citizenship: Origins of Progressivism in Wisconsin, 1885–1900* (1972), presented persuasive evidence that in the late 1890s urban tax issues transformed Wisconsin mug-wumps, many of whom were "conservative businessmen," into "crusaders against corporate arrogance." The most comprehensive account of state and local tax reform between the Civil War and World War I is Clifton K. Yearley's *The Money Machines: The Breakdown and Reform of Governmental and Party Finance in the North, 1860–1920* (1970). Like Thelen, Yearley emphasized the support for tax reform among urban property owners. By contrast, John D. Buenker, in *Urban Liberalism and Progressive Reform* (1973), found strong support for tax reform among Democratic "representatives of the urban new stock working class." Buenker is not clear as to the possible overlap between "working class" and the "urban middle class," but like Brownlee, Thelen, and Yearley, he emphasizes the play of democratic forces. Morton Keller, in *Regulating a New Economy: Public Policy and Economic Change in America, 1900–1933* (1990), reinforces this general view by finding that "a welter of conflicting goals and interests determined tax policy and practice" in cities and states during this period.[33]

---

[33] W. Elliot Brownlee, *Progressivism and Economic Growth: The Wisconsin Income Tax, 1911–1929* (Port Washington, N.Y.: Kennikat Press, 1974);

Recent scholarship focused on federal income taxation—from
congressional proposal of the Sixteenth Amendment in 1909
through World War I—also supports democratic institutionalism.
John D. Buenker's *The Income Tax and the Progressive Era*
(1985), which is the standard source on the movement to ratify
the Sixteenth Amendment, discovers broad-based, democratic support for income taxation within the nation's cities. W. Elliot
Brownlee's essays emphasize all of the elements of democratic
institutionalism in World War I taxation. Another study that ap-
preciates the role of political contingencies, and the radical thrusts
of Congress between 1916 and 1921, is Jerold L. Waltman's *Political Origins of the U.S. Income Tax* (1985).[34]

David P. Thelen, *The New Citizenship: Origins of Progressivism in Wisconsin, 1885–1900* (Columbia: University of Missouri Press, 1972), 202–
22; Clifton K. Yearley, *The Money Machines: The Breakdown and Reform of Governmental and Party Finance in the North, 1860–1920* (Albany: State University of New York Press, 1970), 193–250; John D.
Buenker, *Urban Liberalism and Progressive Reform* (New York: W. W.
Norton, 1973), especially 103–17; and Morton Keller, *Regulating a New
Economy: Public Policy and Economic Change in America, 1900–1933*
(Cambridge, Mass.: Harvard University Press, 1990), 208–15.

[34] John D. Buenker, *The Income Tax and the Progressive Era* (New York:
Garland, 1985); W. Elliot Brownlee, "Wilson and Financing the Modern
State: The Revenue Act of 1916," *Proceedings of the American Philosophical Society* 129 (1985), 173–210; Brownlee, "Economists and the Forma-
tion of the Modern Tax System in the United States: The World War I
Crisis," in Mary O. Furner and Barry E. Supple, eds., *The State and
Economic Knowledge: The American and British Experiences* (Washing-
ton, D.C.: Woodrow Wilson Center Press; Cambridge: Cambridge Univer-
sity Press, 1990; and Brownlee, "Social Investigation and Political Learn-
ing in the Financing of World War I," in Michael J. Lacey and Mary O.
Furner, eds., *The State and Social Investigation in Britain and the United
States* (Washington, D.C.: Woodrow Wilson Center Press; Cambridge:
Cambridge University Press, 1993), 323–64; Jerold L. Waltman, *Political
Origins of the U.S. Income Tax* (Jackson: University Press of Mississippi,
1985).

A few scholars have stressed the importance of democratic idealism to the development of federal taxation after World War I. Benjamin Rader, in an article that deserves greater visibility, pointed to the expression of progressive ideals even in the tax initiatives of the 1920s. R. Alton Lee describes how progressives, into the 1920s, invoked federal taxing power, rather than the commerce clause of the Constitution, to regulate industrial society. Walter Lambert, in an unpublished 1970 dissertation that is the best survey of New Deal tax policy, found that the administration of President Franklin Roosevelt had a deep ethical commitment to the principle of "ability to pay." But the way is open for a substantial democratic-institutionalist history of tax policy between World Wars I and II.[35]

The volume *Funding the Modern American State, 1941–1995: The Rise and Fall of the Era of Easy Finance,* which accompanies the present volume, applies a democratic-institutionalist perspective to the history of taxation since 1941.

In *Funding the American State,* three scholars explore the relationship between the development of post-1941 taxation and the most important objectives of the federal government's tax policies—financing war, financing Social Security, and promoting economic stability. Carolyn C. Jones, a legal scholar, discusses the financing of World War II, the introduction of mass-based income taxation, and the creation of the taxpaying culture that served as the foundation for the mass-based tax. The historian Edward D. Berkowitz examines the development of the financing of Social Security from its origins in 1935 through its dramatic expansion

---

[35] Benjamin G. Rader, "Federal Taxation in the 1920s: A Reexamination," *The Historian* (May 1971); R. Alton Lee, *A History of Regulatory Taxation* (Lexington: University Press of Kentucky, 1973); Walter K. Lambert, "New Deal Revenue Acts: The Politics of Taxation" (Ph.D. dissertation, University of Texas, Austin, 1970).

in 1950–2 and up to the contemporary fiscal crisis. And Herbert
Stein, an economist, brings up to date his classic survey of the
history of fiscal policy, *The Fiscal Revolution in America.*[36]

In *Funding the Modern American State,* two other scholars
focus on the politics of post-1941 tax reform. Julian Zelizer, a
historian, takes up congressional politics. He studies the career of
Wilbur Mills, a longtime chair of the House Ways and Means
Committee (1958–75), and considers Mills's relationship to the
development of a fiscal community that shaped tax policy in the
late 1950s and early 1960s. The political scientist Cathie Jo Martin focuses on the presidency. She explores the dynamic relationships among business interests, the ideas of the business community, and presidential leadership since World War II.[37]

The concluding essay in *Funding the Modern American State* is
an effort by C. Eugene Steuerle, an economist, to apply history to
the forecasting of what is likely to be the next tax regime. He does
this in the context of looking closely at the way in which economic
change can both constrain and create opportunities for new tax
regimes. He concludes that the nation must now do more than
adopt new taxes or shift to a new tax regime in order to fund
programs to meet new social needs. Economic as well as political
conditions dictate, he argues, that the United States adopt a new

---

[36] Carolyn C. Jones, "Mass-Based Income Taxation: Creating a Taxpaying
Culture, 1940–1952"; Edward D. Berkowitz, "Social Security and the
Financing of the American State"; and Herbert Stein, "The Fiscal Revolution in America, Part II: 1964 to 1994"—all in Brownlee, ed., *Funding the Modern American State.* See also Herbert Stein, *The Fiscal Revolution in America* (Chicago: University of Chicago Press, 1969).

[37] Julian Zelizer, "Learning the Ways and Means: Wilbur Mills and a Fiscal
Community, 1954–1964," and Cathie Jo Martin, "American Business and
the Taxing State: Alliances for Growth in the Postwar Period"—both in
Brownlee, ed., *Funding the Modern American State.*

fiscal regime—one that pays for changing priorities, at least in part, by a reallocation of resources from existing governmental programs.[38]

One important episode in post-1941 tax history—the Tax Reform Act of 1986—has received substantial scholarly attention. The scholarship reinforces a democratic-institutionalist framework. Eugene Steuerle's *The Tax Decade, 1981–1990* (1992) stresses two factors that figure centrally in the democratic-institutionalist framework. First, he emphasizes the role of experts, especially the Treasury lawyers and economists (of which he was one), in influencing base-broadening reform in 1986. He argues that they had a coherent vision of reform, derived from the intellectual legacy left by their predecessors within the Treasury. Second, Steuerle emphasizes the way in which economic change—patterns of economic growth and inflation—structured the post-1941 tax regime. Strong support for Steuerle's analysis is found in the book by political scientists Timothy J. Conlan, Margaret T. Wrightson, and David R. Beam, *Taxing Choices: The Politics of Tax Reform* (1990). In addition to the role of the president, the Treasury experts, and their ideas in 1986, Conlan and his colleagues identify the role of congressional entrepreneurs such as Senator Bill Bradley, who acted as brokers between professional experts and the larger political arena, and the media, which enabled the "policy entrepreneurs" to build public support for reform. These political scientists go so far as to claim that the Tax Reform Act of 1986 illustrates that "politics of reform" has now replaced interest-group pluralism. Finally, a first-rate piece of journalism by Jeffrey H. Birnbaum and Alan S. Murray, *Showdown at Gucci Gulch: Lawmakers, Lobbyists, and the Unlikely Triumph*

---

[38] C. Eugene Steuerle, "Financing the American State at the Turn of the Century," in Brownlee, ed., *Funding the Modern American State*.

of Tax Reform (1987), documents the contribution of experts, concepts of tax equity, presidential leadership, and historical contingency to the passage of the 1986 act.[39]

Despite the recent scholarship, much remains to be done before we have an adequate understanding of the nation's fiscal history. We lack modern histories of tariffs and excise taxes, which remained dynamic sources of revenue well into the twentieth century. A comprehensive history of property taxation would tell us not only about the nation's fiscal systems but about its political culture. There is no modern history of the single-tax movement. We lack any substantial histories of taxation during the Civil War or World War II, and much remains to be explored with regard to taxation during World War I and the New Deal. We have no histories of the administration of income taxation, and only a preliminary understanding of its relationship with the cultural dimensions of taxpaying. We have no analytical histories of central institutions in the formation and administration of federal tax policy such as the Department of the Treasury, the Bureau of Internal Revenue, the House Ways and Means Committee, and the Senate Finance Committee.[40]

[39] C. Eugene Steuerle, *The Tax Decade, 1981–1990* (Washington, D.C.: Urban Institute Press, 1992); Timothy J. Conlan, Margaret T. Wrightson, and David R. Beam, *Taxing Choices: The Politics of Tax Reform* (Washington, D.C.: Congressional Quarterly Press, 1990); and Jeffrey H. Birnbaum and Alan S. Murray, *Showdown at Gucci Gulch: Lawmakers, Lobbyists, and the Unlikely Triumph of Tax Reform* (New York: Random House, 1987). The leading proponent of a "politics of reform" analysis is James Q. Wilson. See *The Politics of Regulation* (New York: Basic Books, 1980).

[40] There are, however, excellent reference works written within two of these institutions. On a Treasury bureau, see Jeffrey A. Cantor and Donald R. Sabile, *A History of the Bureau of the Public Debt: 1940–1990 with Historical Highlights from 1789–1939* (Washington, D.C.: U.S. Government Printing Office, 1990). A useful older survey of Treasury borrowing

Modern scholarship on the history of taxation might well contribute to public discourse on the fiscal condition of the nation. A firmer understanding of the nation's fiscal history could help policymakers to identify the possibilities and constraints that must be taken into account in evaluating, and reforming, the ways in which the nation pays for government. The nation is almost certainly coming to the end of the post-1941 regime, and we need, in particular, a comprehensive history of the "era of easy finance" to help guide the development of a new tax regime.

is Robert A. Love, *Federal Financing: A Study of the Methods Employed by the Treasury in Its Borrowing Operations* (New York: Columbia University Press, 1931). On another arm of the Treasury, see Shelley L. Davis, *IRS Historical Fact Book: A Chronology, 1646–1992* (Washington, D.C.: U.S. Government Printing Office, 1992). On the House Ways and Means Committee, see Donald R. Kennon and Rebecca M. Rogers, *The Committee on Ways and Means: A Bicentennial History, 1789–1989* (Washington, D.C.: U.S. Government Printing Office, 1989).

Index